Breakthrough of Spiritual Strongholds

Ending Cycles of Pain

Bill Vincent

© 2013 by Bill Vincent.

All rights reserved. No part of this book may be reproduced, stored in a retrieval system or transmitted in any form or by any means without the prior written permission of the publishers, except by a reviewer who may quote brief passages in a review to be printed in a newspaper, magazine or journal.

Softcover 978-1542491570

PUBLISHED BY REVIVAL WAVES OF GLORY BOOKS & PUBLISHING

www.revivalwavesofglory.com

Litchfield, IL

Printed in the United States of America

Table of Contents

Chapter One Foundations of Strongholds 4
Chapter Two Breaking the Cycle of Pain 11
Chapter Three Breaking Free of Loss 20
Chapter Four Breakthrough is Coming 27
Chapter Five Christian Curses 32
Chapter Six The Enemy's Plan 46
Chapter Seven Guard Your Spirit 62
Chapter Eight Prosperous During Days of Darkness 76
Chapter Nine Solutions to Miracles 87
Chapter Ten No to Witchcraft 93
Chapter Eleven Learning Obedience God's Way 102
Chapter Twelve Cast All Your Cares 108
Chapter Thirteen Our Spiritual Identity 125
Chapter Fourteen Identity Remedies 131
Chapter Fifteen Changing Your Current Situation 138
Chapter Sixteen Satan's Open Door 150
Chapter Seventeen The Sea of Fear 163
Chapter Eighteen Take Off Offense 165
Chapter Nineteen Rebellion is Witchcraft 175
Chapter Twenty The NEW Bride of Christ 187
Chapter Twenty One The Valley of Brokenness 194
Chapter Twenty Two When the Thief Steals 201
About the Author 208
Recommended Books 210

Chapter One
Foundations of Strongholds

Where to begin? Let's start with some foundational things to begin to break the power of the enemy. It doesn't make any difference what race or social status one may have. It doesn't make any difference how long they've been Christians, or what their position is in ministry within the Body of Christ. Many have found their whole life has been a life of pain, disappointment, anger, abandonment, and rejection. Very few have hope that they will ever, ever make it into a place of safety. Most people live at the ends of their ropes. We see them coming to this other place where they begin to cry out to the Lord in the midst of their trouble. What I've found is very few people are willing to face what it takes to cross over, to ride out the storm of life, their wave, and have enough courage to position them for whatever it takes to make it to safe harbor. It takes guts to look into the face of fear and make the choice to live and not die. It is the strongholds of our emotions that often keep us in the rough seas. Strongholds that speak to you, telling you that you will never make it.

For many of us, facing our wound is the most dangerous thing we've ever done. We've spent a lifetime sedating our wounds with drugs, alcohol, or with immorality. This counterfeit way of meeting needs will never bring you to a point of overcoming and being the champion you were designed to be. It is in our beginning the process that allows us to overcome and break free and discover the real heroes within ourselves. It is the process of understanding why we act the way we do (our wounds) and dealing with our habitual behaviors, the strongholds of thinking, and acting on those thoughts of destruction. For those of us in the Church that are really spiritual with religious activity, we try to perform enough to earn God's love.

WAYS STRONGHOLDS ARE BUILT

Strongholds can be passed down from generation to generation through the iniquities of our forefathers. When we allow negative strongholds of thinking to cause us to make choices that wound our families, these choices can become sin.

Exodus 20:5 Thou shalt not bow down thyself to them, nor serve them: for I the LORD thy God *am* a jealous God, visiting the iniquity of the fathers upon the children unto the third and fourth *generation* of them that hate me;

Exodus 34:7 Keeping mercy for thousands, forgiving iniquity and transgression and sin, and that will by no means clear *the guilty;* visiting the iniquity of the fathers upon the children, and upon the children's children, unto the third and to the fourth *generation.*

But how many people do you know that, when they became born again, change their old habit patterns immediately?

Romans 12:2 And be not conformed to this world: but be ye transformed by the renewing of your mind, that ye may prove what *is* that good, and acceptable, and perfect, will of God.

Many times strongholds are built within us from just living in our father's house. There may have been no apparent wounding, yet we find ourselves living in the same destructive lifestyles of our fathers later in adult years. How many of you know alcoholic people who grew up in alcoholic homes? Did their alcoholic parents cause them to become alcoholics themselves? No one can make you become like your examples in life except for you. The choices are yours. Did growing up in that environment influence or cause you to have an iniquity, toward alcohol? Strongholds can be built from deep hurts that resulted from wounds we received.

Proverbs 17:22 A merry heart doeth good *like* a medicine: but a broken spirit drieth the bones.

Our past experiences with relationships have caused us to draw conclusions about life. These relationships may shape our value system (what we see as right or wrong). They may determine how we interact with people or even with God. They may distort the way we relate to our families. We may begin to see life and others through the lens of how we were treated in our past. We don't need to spend much time in the past, but we do need to understand what may be a root issue as to why we act the way we act today with the goal in mind that our *past no longer should dictate our future*. Refusing to allow a platform where people can deal with their struggles and habit patterns of negative thinking keeps people locked up inside. They are told that as a new creature in Christ they should just get over themselves. This will cause confusion to the person who is really trying to deal with their behaviors and strongholds, especially if one of them is seeking praise from man because this need was never met in childhood.

Strongholds can be built within us through a misrepresentation of love—how we perceive love or rejection. We were created in God's image. God is love. God is light. God is a relational being. We too were created for love and relationships. We were created for love to flow through every fiber of our being.

Often parents express their love by the things they do for us and not by heartfelt expressed love given through words, tones of voice, and touch. This can leave a hidden anger within a person because they feel they have not been given the love they were created to receive, thus creating a love deficit. It has the potential of distorting our view of authority figures in our lives or our view of Father God.

Strongholds can be built within us by judgments or the inner vows we make toward others, God, or ourselves.

Whenever you judge another person out of a deep wound or disappointment, it always comes back to you in one form or another. It is the law of sowing and reaping.

Galatians 6:7-9 Be not deceived; God is not mocked: for whatsoever a man soweth, that shall he also reap. For he that soweth to his flesh shall of the flesh reap corruption; but he that soweth to the Spirit shall of the Spirit reap life everlasting. And let us not be weary in well doing: for in due season we shall reap, if we faint not.

Strongholds can be built within us through the words that people speak over us. There is something very soft and tender inside of a person that can be pierced by words.

Proverbs 18:21 Death and life *are* in the power of the tongue: and they that love it shall eat the fruit thereof.

Words can be like railroad tracks that we seem destined to follow our entire lives. Words can affect us for years to come. If we believe in the prophetic words and those words affecting us for years to come, then why do we find it difficult to believe that negative words spoken into an unhealed heart can also have an effect on us and our outcome? No one wants this to be true, but we have seen it too many times in the people we have ministered to. Again, it goes back to telling a person a lie long enough and they believe it. If we are told every day that we don't finish things or that we are clumsy or put your own word curses here, we tend to follow those words, especially if someone in authority in our lives, like our parents, has spoken them.

Strongholds can be built within us through false doctrine or false teaching. Any teaching that does not represent the Spirit of Christ can become a corporate stronghold. A corporate stronghold is a way of thinking, feeling, or acting that a group accepts as truth. It is built within people one thought at a time until lies or deception become truth to them. They often become a hiding place for demonic oppression.

The Spirit of Christ is grace, mercy, compassion, love, meekness, and lowliness of heart. Christ brings comfort by expressing value to a person. You don't have to do it right all of the time to be loved and honored by Christ. Strongholds can be built within us through our ethnic or cultural backgrounds. Corporate strongholds exist in every culture or ethnic group. They develop over a period of time from a practiced belief or tradition that has been around for ages. People accept that this is the way they are and feel there is not a possibility of change. We must ask ourselves, "Is this personality or character trait like our forefathers or is it like Christ?"

Strongholds are reinforced through our false belief structures.

Proverbs 23:7 For as he thinketh in his heart, so *is* he: Eat and drink, saith he to thee; but his heart *is* not with thee.

Job 3:25 For the thing which I greatly feared is come upon me, and that which I was afraid of is come unto me.

When we allow the accuser to bring our thoughts into self-condemnation and self-judgment, then our emotions will follow our thinking. If our emotions and thinking remain negative, then it will affect how we view life, treat others, and the way we feel about ourselves.

We have also seen this overflow into people's health. Our bodies respond to what we tell them the same way they respond to what we physically feed them. Feed your mind negative thoughts on a consistent basis and your mind will send a message to your body to respond in like manner. Examples include:

1. If we think long enough that we have no value and self-worth, then we will "sell ourselves short," treat ourselves cheaply, and the way we feel will be affected. Thus addictions, self-abuse, or sexual promiscuity can result.

2. If we believe that no one loves or cares about us, then we draw rejection out of people. People end up treating us like we feel about ourselves. Depression and hidden death wishes can result.

3. If we continue to think life is too painful to live and that we just want to go on to be with Jesus, our body can respond to the thoughts of death, and sickness sets in.

Everything dies when we don't feed it. If we can develop a habit of not feeding our negative thoughts and strongholds, they will die. How often do you hear the saying, "All hell has just broken loose"?

Foundational Questions

1. Who in your life have you hurt and wounded from unhealed hurts of your past that have caused you to think and believe lies about how you relate to them?

2. What are the support structures that give life to your own habit patterns of flesh that wound those in your life?

3. What lies have you embraced from word curses that have set you upon your own destination to destruction?

Chapter Two
Breaking the Cycle of Pain

I taught a teaching about the Cycle of Pain and I saw much fruit from it. This Chapter is specifically the reason of writing this book. We all need to break the Cycle of Pain. Giving God a place in your life separates you from the very thing you have desired—someone to love and accept you.

It is in turn is an open door for demonic oppression in your life. For us the cycle continues until somebody in some generation will say no. No more.

There are a few things we will deal with wounding, negative thinking patterns, sin and even disobedience.

DARKNESS DEMONIC OPPRESSION
Life happens and we make decisions from our own pain whether or not we are going to leave a cycle of pain for the next generation.

As you look back on your own personal cycle. Does it look anything like one of pain. When history is written about you, what will it say?

A thought is that someone would be remembered for the pain that they brought into the life of another individual, yet it happens every day. Remember Judas of Jesus' time? He lived to betray the greatest example of love that ever lived in human form. Is there any other memory of Judas?

There are so many people that, because of our proneness toward negative thoughts, remember only what they did rather than what their potential was and who they were created to be. Many of us are not living out our greatest potential because we have absolutely no clue what it is. We have never known because no one has been there to speak life to us. Many of us have grown up in abusive homes, and this has caused us to be comfortable with abusive lifestyles. You think that this is just life or your lot in life. I don't think that the Creator of life ever intended for our lives *not* to be good.

Jeremiah 29:11 For I know the thoughts that I think toward you, saith the LORD, thoughts of peace, and not of evil, to give you an expected end.

2Corinthians 3:18 But we all, with open face beholding as in a glass the glory of the Lord, are changed into the same image from glory to glory, *even* as by the Spirit of the Lord.

Pain leaves wounds and scars that sometimes just cannot be forgotten about. So this pain turns into a cycle of behavior patterns that in turn causes us to become pain for those we love.

I had very dysfunctional behavioral cycles that have caused me to recycle this pain from my family of origin. My entire childhood I was ashamed of my life and my cycle of pain nearly caused me my life.

When we look back at this cycle of pain that starts with the pain of a wound in our lives, we see that most of our wounds can be traced back to our love shortfall. A person can only handle being wounded so many times before their ability to receive love is totally dried up inside of them and they are not able to give love to their own personal families, much less the world. Wounding can cause us to start compacting our hurts, emotions, and feelings. Usually by the age of thirty five or forty, the areas we have found our pain to begin to leak out in our relationships and personality.

Some possible characteristics of wounding are:

1. Withdrawal or Isolation: We begin to cut ourselves out from people, thinking that others are not safe and they are the source of our pain. This is a form of controlling our relationships.

2. Walls of Self-Protection: Guarding ourselves from further hurt. Fear of man and past wounding can cause us to lose trust in our relationship with others.

3. Possessiveness: Bonding to only one or two people. Feeling threatened when others try to enter relationship with our one or two. At times, this leaves the one or two with feelings of being smothered. This can lead to emotionally dependent relationships.

4. Control and Manipulation: Deep inside we become insecure with other people. Because of past wounding, we have to be in control so our life will go better. If we can't control then we cut out intimacy to protect ourselves.

5. Difficulty in Receiving Correction or Instruction: We must trust a person to receive from them. When we have been wounded, we tend to harden our hearts and refuse to submit to any authority. We can become very opinionated and demand our own way.

6. Difficulty in Receiving or Giving Love and Acceptance: We must feel secure with a person in order to love them, but wounding has caused them to feel insecure with most people (so they cannot receive from them). Our heart may have become so hardened by the wounding, that we choose not to express our emotions or feelings.

7. Need for Constant Attention or Recognition: Most of us have a deep need for praise. If not given, then we might withdraw from the relationship.

8. Feel Unloved: When we are not valued in our relationships, we begin to feel betrayed. We can easily become suspicious of others. This can set us up for more rejection and blame shifting.

9. Self-Centeredness: Life and conversation focuses more on our needs, causing a "victim mentality."

10. Pattern or Broken Relationships: Fear of man causes us to become people pleasers—not saying what we feel but saying what others want to hear. Because of our distrust of others in the relationship, it hinders us from bonding in an emotional healthy way.

11. Find Identity in a Group: Finding our acceptance in belonging to this group can lead to becoming trapped in the group. The drug culture, homosexuality, or rebel groups are a few examples of this. You will go where you feel you want. We find it hard to lead because we have learned how to follow more than lead.

12. Judgmental Attitudes: Out of our wounding we begin to build ourselves up by putting others down. We surround ourselves with those who agree with us.

13. Lack Intimacy with God: We may blame God for the wounding that has come to our lives. For us, our feeling toward authority is transferred to God. Our relationship with God then is based on our service because we are trying to be loved more. When we don't feel we have a close sense of His presence, then our efforts become our failures and we begin to feel shame that leads to guilt that causes us to hide from His advances.

14. Fears and Phobias: Wounding has led to the fear of man, rejections, and feelings of being a failure. You are only a failure when you blame others for your mistakes.

Anxieties and panic attacks can begin here. Being wounded can cause us to shut ourselves off to love. When we shut ourselves off to love, the stronghold of thought is built and exalts itself against the knowledge of God. God says that He is love and that we have been made in the image of God.

1John 4:8 He that loveth not knoweth not God; for God is love.

1Corinthians 3:18 Let no man deceive himself. If any man among you seemeth to be wise in this world, let him become a fool, that he may be wise.

We choose to believe the lie that *nobody loves me, I am unlovable* when pain comes into our life. We might then choose to act on this pain and allow sin and disobedience into our lives. When we make a choice to deliberately hurt another person, it is considered a sin. When we try and hide by denying that we did anything. We tend to respond in one of three different roles:

1. Victim: As a victim we are incapable of dealing with wounding so we give into the pain. Wounding then leads to feelings of loneliness, to deep inner pain, to feelings of self-pity, to possible depression, to despair, to life without hope, and finally to thoughts of life being too painful to live (death wishes).

2. Persecutor: As a persecutor we will fight against the wounding through negative emotions and resentment, which leads to bitterness that in turn leads to hatred. Hatred then leads to rebellion against anyone, everyone, and everything, thus causing us to live a life as an abuser, rarely acknowledging a need to change.

3. Rescuer: Wounding creates a deep inner agony. The rescuer will struggle against the wound and become indifferent to the hurt. We will take on a superficial happiness and find recognition in being in the spotlight.

Often we have no need for healing because we have overcome our pain through denial. We need to feel good about ourselves so we can help another deal with their wounds. Not acknowledging our wounds can take us to a place of darkness in our lives. Once we live from that place of darkness, we are totally living from our "flesh man."

For me personally, I think all sin comes from a desire to live or protect my "flesh." We run to a place of isolation or what I call darkness. In other words, our lives revolve around ourselves. "I am the center from which go out my thoughts." What can others do for me? "I am the object and end of my thoughts." They begin with me and end with me. "My own glory is, and ought to be, my chief care." What's in it for me? What draws attention to me? "My ambition, to gather the regards of men to the one center, myself." This is drawing the praise and recognition of men to myself. "*My* pleasure is *my* pleasure." I live for my own comfort and happiness. It doesn't matter how it disappoints or wounds another. "My kingdom is—as many as I can bring to acknowledge my greatness over them." "My judgment is the thoughtless rule of things." This is how I interpret them. Whatever I think is right is right and everyone else is wrong. "My right is—what I desire." My rights are what I am in need of in order to enhance my position and greatness. What do I need to feel better about myself and draw others to me? "The more I am all in all to myself, the greater I am." I think that I'm greater as I'm wrapped up in myself. "I am free with the freedom that consists in whatever I'm inclined to do, from whatever quarter may come the preference." To do my own will is to be free and to live. This is the biblical standard of "not my will, Father, but Yours!"

I close my eyes to the fact that I did not make myself for myself. For us, the more selfish and independent I become, the more freedom and greatness I feel.

2Corinthians 5:17 Therefore if any man *be* in Christ, *he is* a new creature: old things are passed away; behold, all things are become new.

When we live for ourselves, we love Father God not for who He is, but for what He can do for us. This is living life from a total selfish perspective. Living from the cycle of pain at our core keeps us trapped in our life's entanglements. We cannot just deal with one of the issues in the cycle of pain, such as casting out a demon or dealing just with the wounds of our past. But if we can begin a process that deals with the *root issues*, we can then get rid of the behavior and be set free in areas of our lives. I believe that my greatest battle has never been with a demonic power, but instead has been with my "flesh man." It has been my choices that I have made out of comforting my own "flesh" that have most often hindered me from growth and maturity. I want it my way, and my way now. Satan is a defeated foe.

The blood of Christ took care of this. So then why do we continue to see defeated people, defeated in their life circumstances and in relational issues? I think that yes, satan has a plan and his plan is to constantly bombard us with lies of deception, and that as we embrace them and apply them to our lives, we become like them. The way for us to continue to mature in the Lord is for us to bring truth (light) to those areas of our lives where deception is in control. We do this through renewing our minds with the concepts of God's love. This cycle of pain can be broken once we are willing to identify and deal with the wounds that have caused a love deficit in our lives. Becoming willing to deal with the issues so that we can focus on destiny is becoming willing to choose a lifestyle of courage.

Cycle of Pain Questions

1. Can you identify some of the wounded areas of your life that have left you dealing with pain?

2. Name three of the characteristics of wounding that have had an effect on your life.

3. Name some of the negative thinking patterns that you can think of that cause you to close your heart out from receiving love and giving it away.

4. Where was the place you ran to for refuge from the pain and abusive behavior unleashed on you? (Remember, some people run to worldly things to numb their pain, such as pornography, overeating, etc.)

5. Patterns that comprised areas of negative thinking and darkness in a person. Which ones can you identify as a part of your life? And do you have other ones you could name?

6. Can you remember a time in your life that your pain may have caused an area of darkness; and can you forgive the one who brought the pain and shame into your life?

Chapter Three
Breaking Free of Loss

Even the strongest people will seem like there is nothing that fazes them until they experience a loss. There is only so much a person in their life can experience such as you watch the most changed individual, your soul mate and a person loved by the whole world, lay day after day in agonizing pain. It is especially hard after you have prayed for about a thousand people for healing.

Many of us fear death. We fear the realization that we will have to relate well at some point in an eternal relationship with the Father. For those of us still left with a *love deficit* in our lives, this could possibly be a very scary event. We are loved throughout our lives but there are times that love may not have been expressed to us in a way that met our need, thus leaving a wound in our emotions that can cause pain for us and others.

Our image of Father God may be determined by wounding that occurs in our early years from our parents. This wounding is normally the beginning or source of most relationship problems.

Strongholds are developed from our habits (an act repeated so often that it becomes involuntary, there is no new decision of mind each time the act is performed). Strongholds can also be birthed from judgments that have been made when wounding occurs or when the basic needs of life are not met. Every human being has built inside of them basic needs. We all have a need to *feel unconditional love.* Even if we did not act right or perform right, there is this need to be able to feel that we are loved. When we know we are loved and valued by another, we then develop a sense of security. In this place of *security,* our value is expressed through a sense of belonging. Once we feel we are valued by another and are secure in their presence, we will become more secure with people in our lives. This sets us up to be able to embrace their blessings and wisdom, thus having an atmosphere created for us to believe in praise, affirmation, and value.

We were created to live in an atmosphere of *praise, affirmation, and value*. In this type of environment we become aware of our purpose in life. This is the place where we sense a *purpose* from God and make decisions to live our destiny. When these needs are not being met, a wound cuts into the soul of a person. Sometimes, if wounds are not dealt with, *mental strongholds* are developed. Under the negative influence of a stronghold, a breeding ground, a source of all sorts of demonic activity, can begin to live.

Strongholds of negative thinking can actually develop a belief structure that for the wounded person becomes their truth and develops into their life's reality. Many times patterns of thinking become a way of living that will develop in a person's life without them even realizing it. Negative thinking that causes a person to develop negative habit patterns often results in the wounding of those we love. It causes some of the greatest relational problems we face today in our society. Wounding can happen without any true understanding as to why we would intentionally or unintentionally hurt someone, but habit patterns have a life of their own.

Some of the signs of emotionally unhealthy traits are:

1. Selfishness

2. Pleasure-seeking mentality

3. Living in a dream or fantasy world

4. Irresponsibility

5. Disregard of consequences of behavior

6. Lack of self-discipline

7. Depression

8. Phobias

9. Addictions

10. Anxieties

11. Dysfunctional behavior—don't trust, don't talk, and don't feel.

Often these habit patterns of thinking turn into mental strongholds within our minds. Usually, they are developed in our family of origin because of wounds and love deficits we have experienced in that environment.

Now, not only was my dad not there to provide for my emotional needs, but my mom was also gone much of my childhood do to illnesses. I have had much ministry over the loss and the feeling of being abandoned by family as well as by Father God.

Habit patterns of thinking, or strongholds, can be hidden so deep within the subconscious that you are literally not aware of them until you get bumped in your emotions.

Living this lie, which became truth for me—my truth and thus my life's reality—kept me from being able to trust the most important people in my life for years to come: my mom, my wife, my brother, my pastor, and my mentors that came in and out of my life over the years. It seemed to me a steady stream of people in my life that I would never be able to completely trust. If I did let my guard down, I would be disappointed and eventually abandoned. My inability to trust wounded those around me who tried to help me live my life successfully. My stronghold of thinking became, *I will only allow certain people into certain areas of my life*. Those who tried to get close to me could feel this invisible wall, this fortress of lack of trust, and they could only lead me so far before they hit my wall.

I thank God that He sent me my wife Tabitha whom I love and do trust and has shown me that I never really knew love and trust until I married her.

Strongholds are characterized by habit patterns of thoughts that exist in the area of our soul, mind, will, emotions, and personality. They are hidden so deeply within our soul that they have the ability to influence the negative thought patterns of our life. Strongholds are habitual lies that we have embraced at the core of our inner being. They are built by a foundation of lies and half-truths. They have become a fortress of thought that influences the way we respond to the truth about God's character within us. Strongholds are spiritual fortresses of thought where demonic influences may hide and be protected. Any area of darkness within our thoughts is an open door to demonic activity. Satan traffics in darkness.

Strongholds exalt themselves above the knowledge of God and give negative forces a secure place to influence our mind, will, and emotions.

2Corinthians 10:4 (For the weapons of our warfare *are* not carnal, but mighty through God to the pulling down of strong holds;)

Strongholds are wrong motivations and attitudes that protect and defend a person's walk in the flesh. Strongholds can lie so deeply within our soul that we don't recognize them as sin, but instead take on the attitude, "That is the way I have always been. This is the way my family is. It is my cultural or ethnic background. How can I expect to be any different?" Strongholds can keep a person from repentance. Lack of repentance hinders the healing process, thus the habitual fortress of thought is not broken within them. Strongholds have a sick core, much like an infection that needs to be lanced so that the poison can drain and the infected area healed, if the stronghold is not dealt with, twisted thoughts and emotions spread poison throughout the soul.

There is a *purpose behind mental strongholds*. They are there to alienate us from believing we are loved by Father God. Mental strongholds do this in many ways:

1. They produce negative thoughts within us in order to block us

from giving or receiving love.

2. They restrict our knowledge of God.

3. They can give us tunnel vision so we can't see wrong from right.

4. They shape our value system and how we value others.

5. They distort our priorities in life.

6. They hinder us from walking in the truth.

7. They can make straight thinking difficult by guarding our weak spots with false feelings and emotions.

8. They send negative messages to our soul.

9. They cause us to draw negative conclusions regarding how we relate to people.

10. They cause us to do things we don't want to do.

When our thoughts continue to dwell upon feelings of fear, insecurity, unbelief, doubt, lust, control, striving, unrest, bitterness, resentment, criticisms, unforgiveness, or habitual sin, a strong deceiving hold begins to build in us like a fortress.

These responses of our flesh then automatically come forth from the habit structures of thought built within us.

Psalms 112:7, 8 He shall not be afraid of evil tidings: his heart is fixed, trusting in the LORD. His heart *is* established, he shall not be afraid, until he see *his desire* upon his enemies.

Or would I return to old habit patterns of thinking from the pain of my past? It is in our identifying what makes us tick that these behaviors or habit patterns are uncovered so they can be dealt with.

Psalms 139:23, 24 Search me, O God, and know my heart: try me, and know my thoughts: And see if *there be any* wicked way in me, and lead me in the way everlasting.

Chapter Four
Breakthrough is Coming

God is coming upon us with breakthrough in every area of our lives. Goodness is part of God's nature. That's why He heals. He gives good things to those who ask. A new season of breakthrough is upon us.

Exodus 38:18, 19 And the hanging for the gate of the court *was* needlework, *of* blue, and purple, and scarlet, and fine twined linen: and twenty cubits *was* the length, and the height in the breadth *was* five cubits, answerable to the hangings of the court. And their pillars *were* four, and their sockets *of* brass four; their hooks *of* silver, and the overlaying of their chapiters and their fillets *of* silver.

I asked the Lord once, "What is Your glory?" He said, "You cannot have My glory without My goodness." They are one and the same. If God gave you one drop of His goodness, what would you do with it? He said to Moses that He will make ALL His goodness pass before you. It is His kindness manifested in your life. We need a revelation of His goodness. THEN He will proclaim His name by revelation.

Judges 6:1-10 And the children of Israel did evil in the sight of the LORD: and the LORD delivered them into the hand of Midian seven years. And the hand of Midian prevailed against Israel: *and* because of the Midianites the children of Israel made them the dens which *are* in the mountains, and caves, and strong holds. And *so* it was, when Israel had sown, that the Midianites came up, and the Amalekites, and the children of the east, even they came up against them; And they encamped against them, and destroyed the increase of the earth, till thou come unto Gaza, and left no sustenance for Israel, neither sheep, nor ox, nor ass. For they came up with their cattle and their tents, and they came as grasshoppers for multitude; *for* both they and their camels were without number: and they entered into the land to destroy it. And Israel was greatly impoverished because of the Midianites; and the children of Israel cried unto the LORD. And it came to pass, when the children of Israel cried unto the LORD because of the Midianites, That the LORD sent a prophet unto the children of Israel, which said unto them, Thus saith the LORD God of Israel, I brought you up from Egypt, and brought you forth out of the house of bondage; And I delivered you out of the hand of the Egyptians, and out of the hand of all that oppressed you, and drave them out from before you, and gave you their land; And I said unto you, I *am* the LORD your God; fear not the gods of the Amorites, in whose land ye dwell: but ye have not obeyed my voice.

Overcoming Christians

We are looking to become overcomers but as we go through life it seems we get further and further from a victorious life. We are about to see a rise of overcoming Christians. Isn't it true that though we are called to be overcomers, many times we make places to hide in our insecurities and the strongholds in our lives?

When God looked for Saul he was hiding amongst the baggage. I love the book of Judges because time after time Israel cries out and God always brings His Moses or Sampson or Gideon. God hears the cry of His people. The Midianites would steal Israel's harvest – strife, contention, and quarreling. The enemy would leave no fruitfulness or breakthrough and Israel was greatly impoverished.

Many Christians are that way, yet called to be overcomers. There will be a day where the inhabitants of the land will say "I am not sick!" – A day of victory. I'm not talking about one or two people; I'm talking about breakthrough for the body of Christ.

Judges 6:11-14 And there came an angel of the LORD, and sat under an oak which *was* in Ophrah, that *pertained* unto Joash the Abiezrite: and his son Gideon threshed wheat by the winepress, to hide *it* from the Midianites. And the angel of the LORD appeared unto him, and said unto him, The LORD *is* with thee, thou mighty man of valour. And Gideon said unto him, Oh my Lord, if the LORD be with us, why then is all this befallen us? and where *be* all his miracles which our fathers told us of, saying, Did not the LORD bring us up from Egypt? but now the LORD hath forsaken us, and delivered us into the hands of the Midianites. And the LORD looked upon him, and said, Go in this thy might, and thou shalt save Israel from the hand of the Midianites: have not I sent thee?

The sword of the Lord

Have you ever asked, "If the Lord loves me, why is all this happening?" Gideon means "valiant warrior" but it also means "the man that cuts a tree." That is a prophetic picture of breakthrough. It is a warrior spirit. Deliverance comes by the sword of the Lord and of Gideon.

His friend responded,

Judges 7:14-20 And his fellow answered and said, This *is* nothing else save the sword of Gideon the son of Joash, a man of Israel: *for* into his hand hath God delivered Midian, and all the host. And it was *so,* when Gideon heard the telling of the dream, and the interpretation thereof, that he worshipped, and returned into the host of Israel, and said, Arise; for the LORD hath delivered into your hand the host of Midian. And he divided the three hundred men *into* three companies, and he put a trumpet in every man's hand, with empty pitchers, and lamps within the pitchers. And he said unto them, Look on me, and do likewise: and, behold, when I come to the outside of the camp, it shall be *that,* as I do, so shall ye do. When I blow with a trumpet, I and all that *are* with me, then blow ye the trumpets also on every side of all the camp, and say, *The sword* of the LORD, and of Gideon. So Gideon, and the hundred men that *were* with him, came unto the outside of the camp in the beginning of the middle watch; and they had but newly set the watch: and they blew the trumpets, and brake the pitchers that *were* in their hands. And the three companies blew the trumpets, and brake the pitchers, and held the lamps in their left hands, and the trumpets in their right hands to blow *withal:* and they cried, The sword of the LORD, and of Gideon.

2Samuel 5:17-20 But when the Philistines heard that they had anointed David king over Israel, all the Philistines came up to seek David; and David heard *of it,* and went down to the hold. The Philistines also came and spread themselves in the valley of Rephaim. And David enquired of the LORD, saying, Shall I go up to the Philistines? wilt thou deliver them into mine hand? And the LORD said unto David, Go up: for I will doubtless deliver the Philistines into thine hand. And David came to Baalperazim, and David smote them there, and said, The LORD hath broken forth upon mine enemies before me, as the breach of waters. Therefore he called the name of that place Baalperazim.

After any kind of graduation or promotion, the enemy comes to challenge. It is important to record the breakthrough, the testimony. Write it down. When you remember all the things God has done for you that faith accelerates your breakthrough. Write your dreams down, everything the Lord gives you. When the battle is raging, we often go into panic mode and our emotions rage.

David took off his armor and went to the secret place. The key to breakthrough – regardless of what's going on, stop and inquire of the Lord. That is very common in all of David's battles, he strategized. He left the frontlines and said, "Lord, what do you want me to do?" There is a place called breakthrough and the Lord can take you there. Advance quickly, there is a window. The Lord brings breakthrough like a breach in a wall. Breakthrough means to burst out, break down, so that you can break open. Break out of where you are, to advance in the kingdom, all the way through. Increase to scatter.

Now! Press in, and go after it!

Chapter Five
Christian Curses

Whether many believe this or not there are many people that experience what I call Christian Curses. This has been used for years by the most religious.

I understand the expressions of disbelief and skepticism this Chapter will bring. Should we believe that curses are real? The Bible does not teach that a Christian *cannot* curse another Christian; it teaches he *should not!* The inception of a curse may be initiated with some common fleshly attitudes and "minor" sinful thoughts, but that is only the beginning.

Do not be fooled into thinking a curse is merely sinful flesh manifesting itself. Demonic and spiritual, a curse takes on a personality and power straight from the pit of hell. It may start with the flesh, but it quickly escalates into a living, breathing, demonic tool, custom made for any Christian who wants to wield its deadly power against another Christian.

Satan does not care who uses a curse as long as someone employs it for its intended destructive and demonic purpose.

Does the New Testament address this problem? Indeed it does!

Paul issued a stern warning about this very possibility and the consequences of such behavior among Christians. He wrote:

Galatians 5:15 But if ye bite and devour one another, take heed that ye be not consumed one of another.

Webster defines the word "war" as "a state of open, armed conflict between two parties." The fact remains: a Christian can war against another Christian. This "civil war" scenario, where spiritual brother is pitted against spiritual brother, is all too familiar in the body of Christ.

I have had many curses from Pastors, Leaders and Church members. They pray for my life to fall apart; financially, physically and even family curses. No one can pray like that without it being called Christian curses.

Set on Fire by Hell

James 3:8-12 But the tongue can no man tame; *it is* an unruly evil, full of deadly poison. Therewith bless we God, even the Father; and therewith curse we men, which are made after the similitude of God. Out of the same mouth proceedeth blessing and cursing. My brethren, these things ought not so to be. Doth a fountain send forth at the same place sweet *water* and bitter? Can the fig tree, my brethren, bear olive berries? either a vine, figs? so *can* no fountain both yield salt water and fresh.

The tongue is described as:

1. A restless evil

2. A restless mischief

3. An irreconcilable evil

4. An intractable evil

5. An evil incapable of being quieted

All these obvious negative analogies are applied to the Christian tongue and mouth!

James 3:6 And the tongue *is* a fire, a world of iniquity: so is the tongue among our members, that it defileth the whole body, and setteth on fire the course of nature; and it is set on fire of hell.

Even a Christian's tongue can be demonically inspired! The tongue is untamable without God. In speaking blessing or cursing, the tongue releases one of two spiritual forces by bringing either the power of God to bear on any given situation or the power of hell.

Like a key, the tongue can open one of two worlds — the world of light or the world of darkness. The tongue can release:

1. Blessing, or it can release cursing.

2. God, or it can release the devil.

3. Good, or it can release evil.

4. Life, or it can release death.

5. Healing, or it can release hurt.

6. Angels (the messengers of blessing), or demons (the messengers of cursing). Our tongue has the potential to do great

things for God or great things for the devil!

The choice of who our tongue helps — God or the devil — is ours! The tongue acts like a magnet, drawing good or evil — attracting God or the devil. Who and what we attract with our tongue depends on the condition of our hearts. According to the Bible, the tongue and the heart are inseparable friends or violent foes. If our heart is right, our words are right; and if our heart is evil, our words will be evil.

1Peter 3:10 For he that will love life, and see good days, let him refrain his tongue from evil, and his lips that they speak no guile:

Blessing or Cursing?

Our tongue has the potential to do great things for God or great things for the devil!

Psalms 34:13 Keep thy tongue from evil, and thy lips from speaking guile.

Proverbs 18:21 Death and life *are* in the power of the tongue: and they that love it shall eat the fruit thereof.

The Bible teaches that Christians have a supernatural ability to bless others — a genuine gift from God. We say and do it everyday, and so we should. The Bible also teaches that Christians can curse one another. Sadly, we have access to that supernatural ability as well. We can access blessing, and we can access cursing.

Unfortunately, this reality seems to have eluded much of the church. We do not understand this negative side to the power of our tongue as we should.

The tongue, even the Christian tongue, can kill! It's that simple. If there is a heavenly power released when we bless — and there is — then a hellish power is released when we curse.

1. If blessing adds to a life, cursing takes away from a life.

2. If blessing builds up a life, cursing tears down a life.

3. If blessing gets the attention of heaven to bring only good into a Christian's life, then cursing gets the attention of hell to bring only evil into the life of another Christian.

Matthew 12:35-37 A good man out of the good treasure of the heart bringeth forth good things: and an evil man out of the evil treasure bringeth forth evil things. But I say unto you, That every idle word that men shall speak, they shall give account thereof in the day of judgment. For by thy words thou shalt be justified, and by thy words thou shalt be condemned.

For the Christian, there is no such thing as a *neutral* spoken word. His words carry life or death, blessing or cursing, good or evil.

To curse is the direct opposite of "to bless." When we bless, we wish good on another person. We speak words of kindness, directing God's loving grace and power toward a per-son's life.

The intention of a blessing is to see the person's life improve, increase, and develop positively since a blessing is always progressive in nature.

When we bless a person, we "fill that person up" with good things, literally heaping God's goodness on them! Indeed, it is a blessing in itself to bless another. In contrast to this, to curse means to wish harm or disaster. It means malevolent speech, to speak evil of another. The intention of a curse is regressive in nature, that is, to bring about a backward motion, to get worse, to decrease, and to develop that which is negative in a person's life.

When we curse a person; we effectively empty, drain, and exhaust all that is good from that person's life. To curse means to displace a person's sense of well-being, to dislodge blessing, to disrupt, to unsettle, to confuse, and to ignite evil against that person.

Some of the similarities of blessing and cursing are:

1. Both are activated (initiated) and imparted (transferred) through human beings.

2. Both believers and unbelievers seem to have this "ability."

3. Both use various forms of the spoken word to convey their intentions, whether good or evil.

4. Both call upon a supernatural power, a form of spiritual solicitation — one legitimate (blessing), the other illegitimate (cursing).

A curse is a conscious, willful attempt to invoke a higher spiritual power against an individual to at least wish him harm if not actually destroy him.

1. Both remain active and alive, searching for their intended candidate or victim until the blessing or curse is expended or consumed on that person.

2. As a blessing is "sent out" *for* another, a curse can be "sent out" *against* another.

3. Both look for a home, a residence, a place to call their own. A curse by nature is a selfish thing; whereas a blessing by its very nature is totally unselfish in purpose and fulfillment.

A blessing unselfishly wants to impact a life for good, and a curse only wants to impact a life for an evil and selfish end — which is usually, if not always, the destruction of the individual.

Evil Focus

To "curse" is to be devoted — to give oneself to — the destruction of something or someone. To pray against, to oppose without righteous grounds, to wish evil against a person is to "curse" that person. It is an evil focus. Planned, calculated, and contrived, a curse does not happen by accident. A curse is not an innocent, unsuspecting act; forethought is always involved.

A curse is a shrewd, scheming, conniving conclusion to a series of sinful attitudes, words, and actions. To curse someone takes real effort, determination, will power, and desire. Without exception the Bible views a curse as a damnable thing worthy of its evil reputation. Curses are never viewed as harmless or trivial. The Bible neither relegates curses to a mere historical context or dismisses them as irrelevant to today's Christian experience.

Our radical views may try and subdue curses simply to a shell of their original significance throughout history, but the Word of God will not allow this. The Bible does not say that curses have diminished in any way. The Bible believes curses are real — very real. They were real thousands of years ago, and they are real today.

Just ask a Christian who has experienced a personal curse, and he will tell you just how real they are!

Precursors to Cursing

What is a precursor? A forerunner — someone or something that comes before or precedes another person or thing. Before actual cursing takes place, even Christians can speak preliminary words of death against other Christians.

Psalms 10:7 His mouth is full of cursing and deceit and fraud: under his tongue *is* mischief and vanity.

Psalms 36:3 The words of his mouth *are* iniquity and deceit: he hath left off to be wise, *and* to do good.

Psalms 5:9 For *there is* no faithfulness in their mouth; their inward part *is* very wickedness; their throat *is* an open sepulchre; they flatter with their tongue.

Proverbs 12:18 There is that speaketh like the piercings of a sword: but the tongue of the wise *is* health.

Romans 3:13, 14 Their throat *is* an open sepulchre; with their tongues they have used deceit; the poison of asps *is* under their lips: Whose mouth *is* full of cursing and bitterness:

Here is a partial list of precursors to cursing mentioned in the Bible. Remember, these sins of speech take place even in Christians and often lead to cursing:

1. Clamor and evil speaking against other Christians

Ephesians 4:31 Let all bitterness, and wrath, and anger, and clamour, and evil speaking, be put away from you, with all malice:

Titus 3:2 To speak evil of no man, to be no brawlers, *but* gentle, shewing all meekness unto all men.

1Peter 3:10 For he that will love life, and see good days, let him refrain his tongue from evil, and his lips that they speak no guile:

2. Backbiting by Christians

Psalms 15:3 *He that* backbiteth not with his tongue, nor doeth evil to his neighbour, nor taketh up a reproach against his neighbour.

2Corinthians 12:20 For I fear, lest, when I come, I shall not find you such as I would, and *that* I shall be found unto you such as ye would not: lest *there be* debates, envyings, wraths, strifes, backbitings, whisperings, swellings, tumults:

3. Slander against your brother

Psalms 50:20 Thou sittest *and* speakest against thy brother; thou slanderest thine own mother's son.

4. Debates, (verbal contentions), backbitings, whisperings, swellings (gossip) and tumults among Christians

2Corinthians 12:20 For I fear, lest, when I come, I shall not find you such as I would, and *that* I shall be found unto you such as ye would not: lest *there be* debates, envyings, wraths, strifes, backbitings, whisperings, swellings, tumults:

Other precursors to cursing may include: vain talkers, lying lips, talebearers, busybodies, hypocrites, false accusers, and false witnesses — all of which are terms taken from the Bible.

These various kinds of verbal sins set the stage for cursing by the Christian.

The prophet Jeremiah warned us well about the destructive power of words from unsuspecting sources when he said:

Jeremiah 9:4 Take ye heed every one of his neighbour, and trust ye not in any brother: for every brother will utterly supplant, and every neighbour will walk with slanders.

A slanderer is a scandal-monger, a tale-carrier — one who destroys with words. When a Christian curses another Christian, he is speaking nothing short of death over him. Curses take no prisoners!

Jeremiah was warning us about the same precursors to cursing listed above.

The potential to curse increases if we have lived a life full of these sins of the mouth and tongue. The deceitfulness, betrayal, and verbal conspiracies that we enter into against another Christian are nothing short of sin and become the seedbed for spiritually destructive curses. Sins of the tongue — such as slander and tale carrying — make cursing an easy next step. Jeremiah continued his warning when he said,

Jeremiah 9:5 And they will deceive every one his neighbour, and will not speak the truth: they have taught their tongue to speak lies, *and* weary themselves to commit iniquity.

If we as Christians persist in these verbal sins, we teach and train our mouths to sin to such a degree that we can no longer tell the truth! We condition ourselves to lie with our words and do not even realize we have grieved the Holy Spirit and brought evil upon our brother or sister in Christ.

Jeremiah warns us that we as Christians can get to the point where we are out of control with our words. A point of no return may exist where we are literally slaves to our own words at the expense of other Christian lives.

Galatians 5:16-21 *This* I say then, Walk in the Spirit, and ye shall not fulfil the lust of the flesh. For the flesh lusteth against the Spirit, and the Spirit against the flesh: and these are contrary the one to the other: so that ye cannot do the things that ye would. But if ye be led of the Spirit, ye are not under the law. Now the works of the flesh are manifest, which are *these;* Adultery, fornication, uncleanness, lasciviousness, Idolatry, witchcraft, hatred, variance, emulations, wrath, strife, seditions, heresies, Envyings, murders, drunkenness, revellings, and such like: of the which I tell you before, as I have also told *you* in time past, that they which do such things shall not inherit the kingdom of God.

Romans 7:18 For I know that in me (that is, in my flesh,) dwelleth no good thing: for to will is present with me; but *how* to perform that which is good I find not.

As long as the soul (mind, intellect, will, emotion) of a Christian entertains evil thoughts, destructive feelings — and exercises its will against others in an ungodly manner — there will be curses by Christians against other Christians.

Romans 7:18 For I know that in me (that is, in my flesh,) dwelleth no good thing: for to will is present with me; but *how* to perform that which is good I find not.

The soul is an eager partner to cursing because cursing somehow empowers the soul, appealing to its drive for recognition, prestige, and control. Cursing feeds the soul, giving it a false spiritual status — but a status nonetheless. A curse entices the soul, making the soul a close ally in the cursing process because both the curse and the soul benefit.

First, the curse benefits by using the soul as a vehicle to inflict its death blow.

Second, the soul benefits by gaining an outlet or a vent for the pent up, festering, negative, sinful emotions and thoughts it has stifled rather than confessed as sin to God.

As long as Christians have wicked hearts and are not willing to walk in the love of God, there will be curses. Jesus said:

Matthew 12:34, 35 O generation of vipers, how can ye, being evil, speak good things? for out of the abundance of the heart the mouth speaketh. A good man out of the good treasure of the heart bringeth forth good things: and an evil man out of the evil treasure bringeth forth evil things.

The flesh, the soul, and the heart (spirit) can all cooperate with a curse, providing a vehicle through which it reaches out and destroys.

Paul wrote this stern warning about Christian flesh, the Christian soul, and the Christian spirit (heart):

2Corinthians 7:1 Having therefore these promises, dearly beloved, let us cleanse ourselves from all filthiness of the flesh and spirit, perfecting holiness in the fear of God.

There is such a thing as filth of the flesh and the spirit! This filth or contamination of the flesh and spirit of a Christian is where cursing lives.

Galatians 2:20 I am crucified with Christ: nevertheless I live; yet not I, but Christ liveth in me: and the life which I now live in the flesh I live by the faith of the Son of God, who loved me, and gave himself for me.

1Thessalonions 5:23 And the very God of peace sanctify you wholly; and *I pray God* your whole spirit and soul and body be preserved blameless unto the coming of our Lord Jesus Christ.

Ephesians 5:18 And be not drunk with wine, wherein is excess; but be filled with the Spirit;

As a Christian, do you desire to remain free from cursing? What can you do? Keep your flesh on the cross where it belongs; keep your thoughts on the Lord where they belong; and keep your spirit filled with His Holy Spirit, which is where it belongs. It's that simple!

Cursed or not Cursed

People are spirits having a physical experience. Many believers and people in the world think spirits are just in the mind, and they explain it away into unbelief. But now that you are aware of the things on the list, you should pray and seek out guidance of the Lord. Begin the process of closing open portals, casting out all evil and unclean spirits, and anointing your home.

The invisible realm is more powerful than we are in the natural.

Chapter Six
The Enemy's Plan

No matter what God is indeed breaking through the Enemy's Plan. The Mighty God sitting above the heavens and the earth is breathtaking and glorious!

Isaiah 9:6 For unto us a child is born, unto us a son is given: and the government shall be upon his shoulder: and his name shall be called Wonderful, Counsellor, The mighty God, The everlasting Father, The Prince of Peace.

Satan and the fallen angels tried to take the Father's position with a military tactic to bring down the Creator from His throne in Heaven.

Let's not take His Word as a joke. We need to get it together, to heed to what the Lord commands and stay away from the enemy's devices. One of the enemy's schemes, which are one of the most powerful deceptions, is to lead people into thinking he doesn't exist.

1Peter 5:8 Be sober, be vigilant; because your adversary the devil, as a roaring lion, walketh about, seeking whom he may devour:

This is how he deceives us, causing us to think it's merely the person we are dealing with that is the problem, when there is much more influencing that individual.

A lot of religious people have a hard time following the Lord.

Remember the words of the Bible; we must make sure we are doers of the Word and not hearers only, deceiving ourselves. We must follow His Word and do what He instructs us to do.

James 1:22 But be ye doers of the word, and not hearers only, deceiving your own selves.

Luke 6:46 And why call ye me, Lord, Lord, and do not the things which I say?

Hypocrites!

Mattew 15:7-9 *Ye* hypocrites, well did Esaias prophesy of you, saying, This people draweth nigh unto me with their mouth, and honoureth me with *their* lips; but their heart is far from me. But in vain they do worship me, teaching *for* doctrines the commandments of men.

We have to remain in a place of holiness in order to be used by the Spirit of God, to implement righteousness to those walking in error and a different spirit.

These counterfeit delusions of Scripture are close to the words of the Great Architect (God), but those who teach them take away from the Holy Bible to build their case. They become blind guides and heretics, not knowing they are blind and unable to see or grasp the light of the surefire Gospel of Christ. You must relentlessly stay true to the Creator of your youth, weathering the storms of adversity and indifference. The world will mock you, even if you are a businessperson, professional, or churchgoer.

The devil makes no adjustments for you. Whether people say,

Galatians 6:9 And let us not be weary in well doing: for in due season we shall reap, if we faint not.

We who are chosen need to pray, read, fast, and consecrate ourselves to make sure that we are hearing the voice of Heaven and obeying Him. It can be very difficult at times, but we need to stop confessing that it's too hard and that we can't do it. Perhaps, if we refuse to speak this way, our walk might just become a little easier.

Philippians 4:13 I can do all things through Christ which strengtheneth me.

The devil hears us and hangs on to every word that comes out of our mouths; we must make sure we do not become super fluent with our words. He is our enemy, an adversary who tries to bring destruction with all kinds of circumstances to prevent us from going farther.

Proverbs 18:21 Death and life *are* in the power of the tongue: and they that love it shall eat the fruit thereof.

Let me take it further; we need to also speak death! Speaking death to those things that should not be in our lives Guarding Your Heart and Spirit lives will start to improve our spiritual awareness. We will notice that breakthroughs will begin to explode, and we will possess a new fervor, setting us in motion in order to have sweet victories. Speak death to that cancer! Speak death to all destructive relationships and soul ties. In God's eyes, it is very crucial for us to do His will. His plan is so much better than ours.

Do His will at all costs! To God be all the glory and honor! The real question is, are we willing to pay the price? We must never give up on speaking life and death into our volatile situations; then we can watch how the Lord will turn it around for our good.

Unfair Judgments
We are judged for our appearance, the kinds of clothes we wear, the cars we drive, the people we love and speak too, and so forth. This is the heart of satan; he hates the fact that we look, talk, and sound like Jesus Christ. Satan, with all that he has in his arsenal, tries to stop us from speaking God's Word, especially through tough times. He is always on the prowl to destroy us, trying The Counterfeit Christian to send all kinds of harm our way with no remorse in his heart (and believe me, he has no heart).

Christians sometimes don't have even a hint of how to handle his tactical approach, and they give up on God because the fire was too hot to bear. The trials are many and continuous, and as we well know, one trial will end just for another to rise up in its place. Many people become bitter and very angry because of all the unexplainable troubles they have had to endure. We must be careful how we exhibit our anger with others and particularly toward God.

Luke 10:27 And he answering said, Thou shalt love the Lord thy God with all thy heart, and with all thy soul, and with all thy strength, and with all thy mind; and thy neighbour as thyself.

We must be sensitive and obedient when God speaks through His anointed ministers, and we must also learn to heed His still small voice in our prayer closets. This way we can learn when to speak the word and when to retain it as we go forth.

Children of God?

1Corinthians 2:14 But the natural man receiveth not the things of the Spirit of God: for they are foolishness unto him: neither can he know *them*, because they are spiritually discerned.

1John 4:5 They are of the world: therefore speak they of the world, and the world heareth them.

Luke 24:16 But their eyes were holden that they should not know him.

Many don't recognize who we are because they are spiritually dead and their ears are stopped—this verse is still true to this day. When speaking about God and His children, the Bible always uses a symbol of intimacy and relationship, like that of a parent to a child.

Matthew 18:4 Whosoever therefore shall humble himself as this little child, the same is greatest in the kingdom of heaven.

He would not separate His children from Himself or put us into obscure categories. Instead, He encourages His children to walk in the admiration of reading His Word, spending time with Him, loving Him, and ministering His Word to others. But unbelievers do not have any desire to give their lives just yet to the Lord, even though they know in their heart of hearts that they need to. Some are deceived, and this is when prayer comes in.

This is not to condemn anyone, but to cause people to think. Winning an argument is easy sometimes, but it's not worth losing the relationship. Speaking the truth with love and gentleness in humility is the key. We are told to continuously attend church services; we are to assemble ourselves accordingly:

Hebrews 10:25 Not forsaking the assembling of ourselves together, as the manner of some *is;* but exhorting *one another:* and so much the more, as ye see the day approaching.

One aspect of being a true child of God and not a hypocrite is being watchful for the return of Christ:

1Thessalonions 5:4, 5 But ye, brethren, are not in darkness, that that day should overtake you as a thief. Ye are all the children of light, and the children of the day: we are not of the night, nor of darkness.

1John 3:1, 2 Behold, what manner of love the Father hath bestowed upon us, that we should be called the sons of God: therefore the world knoweth us not, because it knew him not. Beloved, now are we the sons of God, and it doth not yet appear what we shall be: but we know that, when he shall appear, we shall be like him; for we shall see him as he is.

The verses above state that those who are not children and do not watch for Christ's return are in darkness—unaware of His coming and understanding. We who are saved are in the light and will watch for His coming. We must guide those who are not strong in the Lord to edify those who are not spiritually mature in God's Holy Word. We must have an understanding, especially toward our own loved ones with much passion, commitment, and constant prayer, no matter who they are or what they've become—family, friends, or even our enemies. It's all about souls and love, loving people into the knowledge of God and the Kingdom of our Lord Jesus Christ and His Spirit, for the rejoicing of His Father.

Proverbs 11:30 The fruit of the righteous *is* a tree of life; and he that winneth souls *is* wise.

James 5:20 Let him know, that he which converteth the sinner from the error of his way shall save a soul from death, and shall hide a multitude of sins.

Luke 15:10 Likewise, I say unto you, there is joy in the presence of the angels of God over one sinner that repenteth.

I am so glad that the blood of Christ has cleansed us from sin, guilt, shame, and the stains of our past, giving us countless reasons to read and obey the Word of the Lord. He wants a real relationship with His children, with no hatred, bitterness, or sinful hearts lurking in our members. He wants us to love each other and to live peaceful lives.

Matthew 5:9 Blessed *are* the peacemakers: for they shall be called the children of God.

God has a big plan for all His children, if we will only heed His voice. He is the only one who brings life, supporting us in all areas of our lives so that we can function and become more like Him every day.

Sons and *daughters* refer to the spiritually mature, but we are all His born-again children as long as we stay obedient to Him and His will. Not according to the abiding of the Law, but rather grace. Simply because we love Him enough to walk in obedience so His will may be accomplished in us. Others outside of this understanding are His creation, and God does love them as well, but for them to earn the title of "Child of God" and enter Heaven, they must be redeemed.

John 3:3 Jesus answered and said unto him, Verily, verily, I say unto thee, Except a man be born again, he cannot see the kingdom of God.

We must come from the darkness into the light, which is Christ. This is not popular coming from the pulpit or certain books, but this is biblical. Many of us have tried everything by our own influence and in the power of the Holy Ghost to be holy and obedient to God. Nevertheless, we must remain open in a state of surrender from our wills for genuine liberation to visit and remain. We must keep that in mind every day for the rest of our lives. Being a Christian is a lifestyle and relationship, not a religion.

Hebrews 13:8 Jesus Christ the same yesterday, and to day, and for ever.

Even God called Jesus, God, in the New Testament, confirming the status of His Son's position, validating who He was to give us strength to continue onward.

Hebrews 1:8, 9 But unto the Son *he saith,* Thy throne, O God, *is* for ever and ever: a sceptre of righteousness *is* the sceptre of thy kingdom. Thou hast loved righteousness, and hated iniquity; therefore God, *even* thy God, hath anointed thee with the oil of gladness above thy fellows.

I know it's comforting and popular to call our loved ones children of God, but according to Scripture, if they have not truly accepted Jesus as Lord, they are not children of God. Not everyone who professes Christ or calls themselves Christians is in right standing with God. When we keep plugging these words into people's minds that do not have Christ the hope of glory living in their hearts, the enemy tends to deceive them into thinking they are God's children. This is how the devil distorts their minds so he can keep them from receiving Jesus as their personal Lord and Savior.

We have to be equipped and prepared for what's ahead of us. Jesus declared that it's the "gift and anointing" that He imparts for the believer to have the power to lead humans to salvation.

2Timothy 3:16, 17 All scripture *is* given by inspiration of God, and *is* profitable for doctrine, for reproof, for correction, for instruction in righteousness: That the man of God may be perfect, throughly furnished unto all good works.

John 15:16 Ye have not chosen me, but I have chosen you, and ordained you, that ye should go and bring forth fruit, and *that* your fruit should remain: that whatsoever ye shall ask of the Father in my name, he may give it you.

No Limits

Christians are the only ones who do not have to work their way into Heaven—unlike the followers of false religions and false gods, who believe in some sort of salvation through works. I am not saying that we shouldn't work; our faith without any works is dead, and works without faith is also dead.

James 2:17, 18 Even so faith, if it hath not works, is dead, being alone. Yea, a man may say, Thou hast faith, and I have works: shew me thy faith without thy works, and I will shew thee my faith by my works.

Romans 14:23 And he that doubteth is damned if he eat, because *he eateth* not of faith: for whatsoever *is* not of faith is sin.

Jesus can do whatever He wants when He wants to do something that glorifies Himself and His Father. Limiting God would be foolish; He is sovereign.

Who's Your Daddy

There are two fathers who exist in our world today, the one in Heaven and the one here on the earth. Father God and the father of lies (as we know, one is real, and the other is a counterfeit).

We must bear the fruit of the Holy Spirit in order to differentiate who is who in these last days. Aren't you blessed that you and I decided to choose God over the devil? This is a blessing beyond human comprehension. I feel a burden and deep concern thinking about loved ones, longing for them to make a decision to accept Christ as their Lord and Savior as I have done. Do not allow yourself to be deceived by the devil and his lies regarding you, and do not believe the lie that it is too late for your family to come to the Lord.

Ready for War

Make sure you put on the whole armor of God. If you do not, the enemy will have a soccer game in your mind. He doesn't play fair; he will make sure you will be open in your spirit for all different kinds of afflictions.

As soon as you go to your place of employment, it will not take long before the devil shows his face.

Here are some tips to help you confess and realize what this armor does for you. The Spirit of God recorded this for a purpose, to help you learn His ways of wisdom.

1. *Helmet of Salvation*—this protects your mind from the fiery darts of the enemy.

Plead the blood of Jesus over your mind (soul), and pray for the helmet of salvation to protect your spirit. The soul and spirit are knit closely together.

Remember, your soul needs to be renewed; your spirit is already saved and becomes a new creation in Christ Jesus.

Romans 12:2 And be not conformed to this world: but be ye transformed by the renewing of your mind, that ye may prove what *is* that good, and acceptable, and perfect, will of God.

If you mix the two, it can lead to confusion, and God is not the author of disorder.

1Corinthians 14:33 For God is not *the author* of confusion, but of peace, as in all churches of the saints.

1Corinthians 14:40 Let all things be done decently and in order.

2. *Breastplate of Righteousness*—this piece of armor protects your heart. The Word states that people have desperate and immoral hearts.

Jeremiah 17:9 The heart *is* deceitful above all *things,* and desperately wicked: who can know it?

God is always looking and examining people's hearts. You must make sure that your heart is protected at all times. It's very important that you do not have unforgiveness or bitterness toward anyone.

This can be a *huge* hindrance in your walk with Christ. Guard your heart, and most of all, forgive everyone.

Proverbs 4:23 Keep thy heart with all diligence; for out of it *are* the issues of life.

3. *Shield of Faith*—this will protect you when hell's agents come your way with a different Gospel message. Make sure you are walking in your faith.

Your faith will please God and will help you overcome the enemy's devices and become acquainted with your exact purpose.

Without *stubborn faith* in Christ, you will leave the Lord and go back to your old ways.

Jesus said that if you leave your faith in God for another, even if it's your own, eight demons will enter into you, and the last state of your life will be worse than the first.

Matthew 12:43-45 When the unclean spirit is gone out of a man, he walketh through dry places, seeking rest, and findeth none. Then he saith, I will return into my house from whence I came out; and when he is come, he findeth *it* empty, swept, and garnished. Then goeth he, and taketh with himself seven other spirits more wicked than himself, and they enter in and dwell there: and the last *state* of that man is worse than the first. Even so shall it be also unto this wicked generation.

Be a watchman, knowing that most times believing has a beginning and an ending; faith always is. I will talk more about that later.

4. *Belt of Truth*—this is similar to the Shield of Faith. Jesus is the truth. As long as He remains wrapped around your waist in the center of your body, you will always retain truth from within the depths of your spirit.

Realize that belts have different levels; so does the truth of His Word. Christians go from glory to glory, faith to faith, and strength to strength.

5. *Sword of the Spirit* (the Word)—the spoken Word will always rebuke, expel, resist, banish, and destroy the works of the devil.

Satan has no place to hide when you speak the eternal Word. The adversary hates it with a passion.

Demons know that the best way to attack believers is by first covering their mouths. The Word cuts both ways, like a two-edged sword; be prepared always, and read your Word on a day-to-day basis.

Hebrews 4:12 For the word of God *is* quick, and powerful, and sharper than any twoedged sword, piercing even to the dividing asunder of soul and spirit, and of the joints and marrow, and *is* a discerner of the thoughts and intents of the heart.

6. *Gospel Shoes of Peace*—the steps of a good man are ordered by the Lord, and He delights in his ways. This piece of armor helps you know where you should and shouldn't go.

Psalms 37:23 The steps of a *good* man are ordered by the LORD: and he delighteth in his way.

When the enemy comes against you and begins to bring chaos into your dwelling, you know how to step on him and bruise his head! He is always going to be under your feet forever! He has no future, but you do.

Trials and Tests

As we know already, tests will come, and that is a promise from the Lord. So we must let our tests become our "testimonies."

The Scriptures are filled with promises to build us up. These promises are not all for our good. Some of these promises have consequences that pertain to breaking the law and bringing death to our doorsteps. Now that I have become wiser, I ask God for His good promises. Allowing the text of His promises to echo from my mouth into the atmosphere of my home creates an environment of tranquility and hope. When we begin to act upon what He has already given us, we will see a variation in our attitudes, particularly when trials come our way. It's a sad thing when people start out good with the Lord and then stop when the trials and tests of every day life come their way. When their faith is challenged, it causes some Christians to lose heart, keeping them from calling out to Jesus for help when they need to. We are nothing without Him.

As if being attacked in the spirit wasn't enough, now here come hell's agents and counterfeit Christians ready to devour us in the natural.

Luke 8:11-15 Now the parable is this: The seed is the word of God. Those by the way side are they that hear; then cometh the devil, and taketh away the word out of their hearts, lest they should believe and be saved. They on the rock *are they,* which, when they hear, receive the word with joy; and these have no root, which for a while believe, and in time of temptation fall away. And that which fell among thorns are they, which, when they have heard, go forth, and are choked with cares and riches and pleasures of *this* life, and bring no fruit to perfection. But that on the good ground are they, which in an honest and good heart, having heard the word, keep *it,* and bring forth fruit with patience.

Chapter Seven
Guard Your Spirit

The reason for writing this Chapter is to prepare the Body of Christ for the coming Messiah. This is to get us all to the Breakthrough of Spiritual Strongholds. You must know who you are in Christ and what you are capable of doing for the Lord while you're here on earth. In order for you to achieve the blessings of God and be victorious, you must follow the path of obedience with humility.

You will hear a lot about the heart, mind, and spirit to help keep you in alignment with the Word of God, positioning yourself to receive the blessings that have been waiting on you. What you are about to hear is going to equip, encourage, empower, edify, correct, instruct, build up, and prepare you to become aware of the enemy's strategies and devious counterfeits, which many times come in the form of people you encounter in your everyday living.

You will know the true meaning of your life in Christ when you keep away from such a crowd. For too long the devil has uprooted and torn down many born-again believers into thinking they are worthless and cannot obtain their true function in life. You were created for more than just going through the motions and hoping that one day things will turn out for your good. Well, your day is *now!*

The enemy's agenda is to bring confusion, striking the weak and fainthearted with all he has, causing believers to lose their route, impeding them from becoming the very thing God has called them to be. In this Chapter, I hope to assist believers in escaping a spirit of unwillingness and equip Christians who have faltered and forgotten who they really are, giving them the proper tools to reach their purpose.

The adversary has determined to target and then assault those who are already in bondage. Therefore, carrying a canopy of blindness with him, he places it over the eyes of Christians to elude them from their promises and the unlimited blessings that God has already stored up for their lives.

Jesus Christ has commissioned me to be His "apostle to the nations," mandating my life with the purpose and plan to bring true righteousness and holiness to the Body of believers in this nation and around the world, preparing them for Christ's imminent return. Like what John the Baptist did for Christ in the First Coming—he prepared the way for the Lord—I shall do for Christ's Second Coming, by His command. I must be obedient.

And in my obedience, I pray that this Chapter and the anointing of the Holy Ghost falls on you as you hear, and when you are finished hearing, may the presence of God flood you with His everlasting love, peace, and grace.

Proverbs 4:23 Keep thy heart with all diligence; for out of it *are* the issues of life.

Comparing the real to the counterfeit tells you a lot about the imitation. The sole purpose of the counterfeit is to fool people into thinking they have equal value to the original. But when we put both the counterfeit and the real into the light, it tends to reveal the original from the imitation. If the replicas do not have the eternal seal, the strip to prove their authenticity, God will cast them into the *lake of fire,* never to be received, heard, or seen again.

Revelations 20:15 And whosoever was not found written in the book of life was cast into the lake of fire.

There are many believers who do not realize the infinite power that lies within the deepest part of who they really are. I pray that, as you hear, your faith will be empowered, becoming sharper and more attentive to the enemy's devices; I pray too that you will come to know your definitive purpose in this life, whether it's through people, the supernatural, or both.

We must continue to believe God. Many have swayed from the Lord and believed life with Christ was not something to be part of. Christians who once were on fire for God have given up or, worse, have committed suicide. Countless others in the faith and in the world have been deceived. They have been lured away from the truth of God's Word by the so-called "good things" of this world, its system, and its beliefs.

Many have given into false hopes, visions, and dreams that promise new life, lots of money, or certain freedoms; but in the end, these counterfeits only end up destroying people's lives, sometimes slowly, sometimes quickly. The message I bring to you is reassurance, that the plan Christ has for you is greater than you can ever ask or think. I also want you to be aware of others who claim to be "saved and sanctified." They claim to be filled with the Holy Spirit, and some are filled truly, but they are engaged with a spirit that is not holy. As a matter of fact, whether or not a person is truly saved and sanctified is a heart and spirit issue most of the time. Many concentrate on the mind, but the heart, the spirit, and the devil also need to be dealt with; otherwise we could find ourselves in unfathomable trouble.

As we all know, there are many thoughts running around in the minds of believers. We must be thorough in how we confess those things into our environment, especially with other individuals inside and outside of our comfort zones.

Matthew 12:34 O generation of vipers, how can ye, being evil, speak good things? for out of the abundance of the heart the mouth speaketh.

Proverbs 23:7 For as he thinketh in his heart, so *is* he: Eat and drink, saith he to thee; but his heart *is* not with thee.

Matthew 6:21 For where your treasure is, there will your heart be also.

What we don't hear from the ear of our hearts, too often, is the fact two plans are available to humankind. God has a plan for our lives, and the devil also has a plan for our lives.

One is for our destruction, and the other is for our good, unto life eternal. The lie of the devil is to steal our dreams, kill our relationships (engagements, marriages, friendships, business partnerships, and the like).

Job 1:7 And the LORD said unto Satan, Whence comest thou? Then Satan answered the LORD, and said, From going to and fro in the earth, and from walking up and down in it.

1Peter 5:8 Be sober, be vigilant; because your adversary the devil, as a roaring lion, walketh about, seeking whom he may devour:

This is why we must always be prepared spiritually and naturally, making sure when we start our hand-to hand combat, which is prayer, that we can go to war with assurance, boldness, and holiness in the power of the Holy Ghost.

If you have no prayer life with God, the enemy will mock you, and you will become an easy target. Remember, beloved, without a prayer life, your walk with Christ will be very short and will slowly fade and diminish. You have to pray every single day for the rest of your life. You cannot give up because satan is not giving up on you until you are gone from this life. He wants to make sure that God is nowhere to be found in your everyday thoughts.

John 10:10 The thief cometh not, but for to steal, and to kill, and to destroy: I am come that they might have life, and that they might have *it* more abundantly.

Ephesians 6:12 For we wrestle not against flesh and blood, but against principalities, against powers, against the rulers of the darkness of this world, against spiritual wickedness in high *places*.

2Corinthians 10:4-6 (For the weapons of our warfare *are* not carnal, but mighty through God to the pulling down of strong holds;) Casting down imaginations, and every high thing that exalteth itself against the knowledge of God, and bringing into captivity every thought to the obedience of Christ; And having in a readiness to revenge all disobedience, when your obedience is fulfilled.

2Corinthians 4:3, 4 But if our gospel be hid, it is hid to them that are lost: In whom the god of this world hath blinded the minds of them which believe not, lest the light of the glorious gospel of Christ, who is the image of God, should shine unto them.

Here are several Scriptures you can pray to speak against the enemy and to guard your heart, mind, and spirit:

Isaiah 54:17 No weapon that is formed against thee shall prosper; and every tongue *that* shall rise against thee in judgment thou shalt condemn. This *is* the heritage of the servants of the LORD, and their righteousness *is* of me, saith the LORD.

Job 40:9 Hast thou an arm like God? or canst thou thunder with a voice like him?

Luke 1:51 He hath shewed strength with his arm; he hath scattered the proud in the imagination of their hearts.

2Chronicles 20:15 And he said, Hearken ye, all Judah, and ye inhabitants of Jerusalem, and thou king Jehoshaphat, Thus saith the LORD unto you, Be not afraid nor dismayed by reason of this great multitude; for the battle *is* not yours, but God's.

Exodus 15:6 Thy right hand, O LORD, is become glorious in power: thy right hand, O LORD, hath dashed in pieces the enemy.

Ephesians 6:10 Finally, my brethren, be strong in the Lord, and in the power of his might.

Deuteronomy 33:27 The eternal God *is thy* refuge, and underneath *are* the everlasting arms: and he shall thrust out the enemy from before thee; and shall say, Destroy *them*.

Zechariah 4:6 Then he answered and spake unto me, saying, This *is* the word of the LORD unto Zerubbabel, saying, Not by might, nor by power, but by my spirit, saith the LORD of hosts.

Counterfeits

Christians come in all different forms. *Counterfeit* means "to imitate, to forge, and to simulate." In these last days, numerous people will admit to being on the side of God. These people may be relatives, followers of other religions, friends, or associates you highly respect.

It's very important to have this discernment, especially when we have individuals from all areas of life come into our circles. We cannot *always* have people touch us, pray for us, and give us words.

1Timothy 5:22 Lay hands suddenly on no man, neither be partaker of other men's sins: keep thyself pure.

This is not to say we should make everyone we encounter feel uncomfortable and offended. But we should be discerning and aware of our surroundings—aware of whom is surrounding us, like watchmen or seers, a type of prophet according to the Bible.

If we don't walk in the Spirit with discernment, we will be inviting all different kinds of spirits into our homes. Demonic spirits are spiritual hitchhikers. They cling to the ignorant, and they follow, sleep, and hunt the weaker ones in the faith.

Hosea 4:6 My people are destroyed for lack of knowledge: because thou hast rejected knowledge, I will also reject thee, that thou shalt be no priest to me: seeing thou hast forgotten the law of thy God, I will also forget thy children.

If you do not know how to Guard Your Heart and Spirit, have the gift of discerning of spirits, or if you do have it, but do not know how to use it, pray and ask the Lord for help.

If you do not take this seriously, the outcome can be devastating; people without knowledge will start transferring spirits one to another. This is dangerous to the believer and the Church. Please be very careful as the days begin to engulf the world with evil. When you relate with believers or sinners, or when you are making home and hospital visits, pray and anoint yourself with oil if you do not know the people you are dealing with. Protect your spirit with the Word of God to make sure your spirit and mind do not wander into places they shouldn't. Guard your gates (ears, eyes, nose, and so forth), because it is not always easy to see when spirits try to attack you or attach themselves to you (thus the importance of discerning spirits). You must guard your gates because unclean spirits can enter through your nose and mouth, and when they are cast out, they come out where they entered.

Proverbs 4:7 Wisdom *is* the principal thing; *therefore* get wisdom: and with all thy getting get understanding.

Some physical ailments are actually spiritual, but it boggles the human mind and is, therefore, categorized by doctors as unexplainable. This same reliance on human understanding causes people to be unaware that demons travel and follow people around in the spirit, harassing them. Sometimes this happens on a day-to-day and night-after-night basis, while people have no clue what is really going on with them, their household, or their children.

Sometimes we may become frustrated, feel angry, get headaches, feel sick all of a sudden, or spit up blood. This is a spirit of witchcraft, anger, a strong fence of warlockism, rebellion, and stubbornness that is coming against us. Some people experience these things as they lack prayer—almost an inability to pray. They know they need to pray, when they feel the unction of the spirit, it's like they are being squeezed, and it affects their prayer lives.

Acts 16:16 And it came to pass, as we went to prayer, a certain damsel possessed with a spirit of divination met us, which brought her masters much gain by soothsaying:

This spirit of python slithers its way into Christians' and unbelievers' heads, wrapping itself with the objective of constricting and choking the Word of God and prayer out of their hearts and minds, causing them to be unfruitful and lacking. You can read even more about this spirit and many in my book Defeating the Demonic Realm.

(We must come against it and fight back, keeping the Word with all that is within us, because the end is near.)

Matthew 13:22 He also that received seed among the thorns is he that heareth the word; and the care of this world, and the deceitfulness of riches, choke the word, and he becometh unfruitful.

Luke 8:14 And that which fell among thorns are they, which, when they have heard, go forth, and are choked with cares and riches and pleasures of *this* life, and bring no fruit to perfection.

In the days we live in, this python spirit is *one* of countless spirits that causes us to struggle to read God's Word and pray. When we are about to open up our Bibles and read, we may not know what to read, and we experience all sorts of interruptions coming in every direction. The baby cries, the kids start fighting, the phone rings, and so forth—disruption surrounds us all. This proves that there is a spiritual war that is beyond all of our imaginations combined, and it is happening in the supernatural realm.

Unfortunately, a lot of believers do not believe in the spiritual realm, denying that hell or the devil even exists. Of course, God is more powerful than anything in existence (He is the Creator of all things), but we do not want to be ignorant of the fact that evil spirits exist.

It's Time to Clean House

Demonic spirits occupy the first and second heaven, which is our atmosphere, as well as where the Sun, Moon, and Stars reside.

For those who need guidance in order to realize what is necessary, I have listed some reasons why these attacks occur:

1. *Living in disobedience or partial obedience*: which means an individual is not truly taking the Word of the Lord at its full potential seriously, and only obeying parts of it, or none at all.

2. *Unawareness/ignorance*: It's no excuse not to be aware of God and His ways. You must become aware and disregard that ignorance is bliss.

3. *Participating in necromancy*; contact with practicing mediums, sorcery, even speaking to the dead.

4. *Use of white and black magic* (through witches and warlocks).

5. Use of demonic video games, movies, certain television shows, and anything else that may welcome evil spirits to have entry in your life and home.

6. Involvement in false religion, including idol figures, or figurines, even your worship of such things.

7. Involvement with Santeria, witchcraft, Wicca, or Voodoo, whether it be out of curiosity or because friends have influenced you to dabble in it.

8. Use of demonic books, statues, pictures/ images, or Ouija boards.

9. Generational curses, pride, or the spirit of leviathan, which is a stronger pride of haughtiness operating in and through your life.

10. Familiar spirits: things which are recognized by family and friends that may have access in your life. Such as: mediums, witches, wizardry, sorcery, alcoholism, loose living, drugs, etc.

Leviticus 19:31 Regard not them that have familiar spirits, neither seek after wizards, to be defiled by them: I *am* the LORD your God.

Isaiah 19:3 And the spirit of Egypt shall fail in the midst thereof; and I will destroy the counsel thereof: and they shall seek to the idols, and to the charmers, and to them that have familiar spirits, and to the wizards.

11. Desert spirits, animal spirits, or animal sacrifices

Isaiah 34:11-15 But the cormorant and the bittern shall possess it; the owl also and the raven shall dwell in it: and he shall stretch out upon it the line of confusion, and the stones of emptiness. They shall call the nobles thereof to the kingdom, but none *shall be* there, and all her princes shall be nothing. And thorns shall come up in her palaces, nettles and brambles in the fortresses thereof: and it shall be an habitation of dragons, *and* a court for owls. The wild beasts of the desert shall also meet with the wild beasts of the island, and the satyr shall cry to his fellow; the screech owl also shall rest there, and find for herself a place of rest. There shall the great owl make her nest, and lay, and hatch, and gather under her shadow: there shall the vultures also be gathered, every one with her mate.

12. Refusal to believe that satan exists is one of the most popular in the secular world. Most believe the devil is a figment of our imagination. We must know that the Bible clearly states he and his fallen ones exist.

Revelations 12:9 And the great dragon was cast out, that old serpent, called the Devil, and Satan, which deceiveth the whole world: he was cast out into the earth, and his angels were cast out with him.

13. Rejection of Jesus Christ as Lord and Savior is one main reason for multitudes to be cast out from God's presence

John 3:3 Jesus answered and said unto him, Verily, verily, I say unto thee, Except a man be born again, he cannot see the kingdom of God.

Matthew 8:12 But the children of the kingdom shall be cast out into outer darkness: there shall be weeping and gnashing of teeth.

14. Interaction with spiritual birds or fowl allowed to enter into the arena of your inner circle can also be very dangerous.

Guard your gates at all times so you will not be ensnared.

Ecclesiastes 9:12 For man also knoweth not his time: as the fishes that are taken in an evil net, and as the birds that are caught in the snare; so *are* the sons of men snared in an evil time, when it falleth suddenly upon them.

Chapter Eight
Prosperous During Days of Darkness

We are approaching the greatest time of all. Where God shall reveal Himself more and darkness shall have its last rise. The purpose God is doing is to quicken desire and vision for the end-time mandates and cooperate with the Holy Spirit in our preparation. This is perhaps the most important generation in human history, and comparable in importance with the day of the Lord's death and resurrection.

These are both sobering and exciting times requiring our full attention and sincere responses.

Vessels of Honor

But in a great house there are not only vessels of gold and silver, but also of wood and clay, some for honor and some for dishonor. Therefore if anyone cleanses himself from the latter, he will be a vessel for honor, sanctified and useful for the Master, prepared for every good work.

2Timothy 2:20, 21 But in a great house there are not only vessels of gold and of silver, but also of wood and of earth; and some to honour, and some to dishonour. If a man therefore purge himself from these, he shall be a vessel unto honour, sanctified, and meet for the master's use, *and* prepared unto every good work.

The end-time scenario is taking shape and the players are starting to take their position in the dramatic unfolding of events prophetically observed by prophets throughout history. Hunger and desire to become vessels of honor is being imparted to those given the opportunity to participate.

It is our prayer that each person will respond with favor and give the Holy Spirit permission to fully clothe them with Himself, making us the instruments of His warfare and useful to the Master for every good work. The Scriptures clearly outline, directly and through types and shadows, the consecration and sanctification necessary to become vessels in whom the Lord will find His rest and through whom He will do His greater works.

From among the various redemptive names illustrated in the Old Testament, Jehovah Shammah---The Lord Who is Present, is the one with highlighted emphasis for this hour. When the promise of this redemptive name is realized, the Lord is fully present bringing with Him all of the other redemptive attributes inherent in His nature. The Lord is our— Provider, Healer, Banner, Sanctifier, Peace, Shepherd, Righteousness, Recompense, Defense as the Lord who smites, and the Lord of Hosts orchestrating the armies of God providing a canopy of protection around those who are His sons and daughters. All of His attributes will be on display in amplified form during our watch.

An Invitation

There is a flourishing sense of anticipation and purpose concerning the days in which we are living. The marked increase in the intensity and focus within many Christians relates to the birthing of Kingdom purposes in our nation and throughout the earth. Some individuals are experiencing measures of increase in anointing and various expressions of outpouring to quicken and prepare us for the next wave of the Spirit.

Revelations 4:1 After this I looked, and, behold, a door *was* opened in heaven: and the first voice which I heard *was* as it were of a trumpet talking with me; which said, Come up hither, and I will shew thee things which must be hereafter.

The objective and commission given to us as individuals is to understand spiritually the mysteries associated with these great truths and convey them to the body of Christ. That is the hopeful aspiration of this book; to awaken God's people to their destiny and create desire to be groomed for their purpose. We must see Breakthrough of Spiritual Strongholds as we walk into this next level.

Jeremiah 33:3 Call unto me, and I will answer thee, and shew thee great and mighty things, which thou knowest not.

The truths associated with this reality are quite significant and provide keys that unlock prominent mysteries of Heaven's Kingdom. Many individuals allowed this experience must go through the preparation and refining described in this book and essential for this weighty responsibility. It is difficult to adequately express the importance of being clothed with the garment of humility in the execution of this commission and the sharing of great mysteries imparted in this hour.

God's Love

There will be many who will be allowed to go behind the veil, to obtain and experience expressions of God's Divine love that will transcend anything that we presently know. It will be a greater comprehension of His love and Heavenly design for us and also a fulfillment of scripture.

John 17:26 And I have declared unto them thy name, and will declare *it:* that the love wherewith thou hast loved me may be in them, and I in them.

His love for us will supply the essential spiritual provisions necessary to see us through to our promises. This central truth is an emphasis of the Holy Spirit pointing us to a form of genuine unity with Him that will also birth in us brotherly love and fraternal affection. Jealousy and selfish ambition have no place in the joining of individuals and ministries for the purpose of pursuing a higher mandate and greater fruitfulness during the end-time generation.

Throughout the church there is an aligning of people and ministries that will produce a much higher anointing and authority in the realm of the Spirit.

Mandate of Breakthrough

Clearly, there are many purposes for which we are being equipped and prepared. However, three notable divine mandates begin to emerge as our primary focus. Our highest purpose and the one instrumental in allowing us to achieve all others purposes and mandates, is to know God as personally and intimately as He may be known. There is an open door and a call to come up higher to a place of fellowship and exchange with the Creator and establish friendship with God. From that place of communion we begin to receive the unveiling of His nature and attributes as not merely intellectual perceptions but the revelation and comprehension of His Person. It was Isaiah's great privilege to see Heaven's design before the throne of God; there Seraphim spoke one to another declaring "Holy, Holy, Holy is the Lord of Hosts." They were allowed to see with their eyes demonstrations of His majesty and authority and give expression to it. Their words began to fill the temple with smoke and Glory by witnessing with their eyes and expressing with their lips the revelation of God sitting upon His throne in absolute and perfect supremacy and sovereignty.

As the Seraphim gave Glory to Him and He received the Glory due Him, more of his Divine attributes began to be revealed causing an even greater expression of praise and Glory. This Kingdom exchange and heavenly design continued filling the atmosphere with the Glory and illumination of God until the entire temple was saturated with the appearance and revelation of His Glory. That is the fashion of Heaven that is to be transferred to the earth; our second end-time mandate to create an atmosphere on the earth that is consistent with His nature and character in which He can dwell. If we can fulfill this mandate, all the other purposes and desires for which we long will naturally be established and achieved by His Presence and anointing resting in us.

We must become the instruments that create a similar atmosphere on earth so He can tabernacle in us and accomplish all that He has foretold for this generation. The third mandate for winning the lost and healing the sick will take place because of the evidence of God's Glory resting on the Lord's friends experiencing close encounters with Him. We are given the incredible opportunity in this generation to function under the principles of the Kingdom of Heaven and experience intimacy with God and demonstrate the powers of the age to come.

Satan's strategies,

Not to Move Forward Because of Fear

Why are most people not pressing in to all that God has for them? A major reason is fear. A strategy of Satan is to get you to hold back because of fear. This could be fear of failure, fear of succeeding, fear of rejection, fear of man, being left etc..

I meet people all the time who are afraid to make decisions because they fear that they will be wrong or that it will be outside of God's timing. This causes them to stay in a neutral position in life. This is exactly where Satan wants you to stay. You might have a good intention of making the right choices, but not making decisions is not the solution.

The fact is that we all learn by mistakes and God does not mind you making a few if your intent is not evil. We all have some type of fear in our lives and the funny part is that the fear is not usually based in reality. You can recognize when you or someone you know has fear just by the way you talk and view life.

If you find yourself using words like, "I'm afraid, I would be scared, that terrifies me ..." then you probably have a good amount of fear that is most likely holding you back in some area of your life. The words "do not be afraid" appear in the Bible nearly over sixty times. That's a lot.

Isaiah 43:1, 2 But now thus saith the LORD that created thee, O Jacob, and he that formed thee, O Israel, Fear not: for I have redeemed thee, I have called *thee* by thy name; thou *art* mine. When thou passest through the waters, I *will be* with thee; and through the rivers, they shall not overflow thee: when thou walkest through the fire, thou shalt not be burned; neither shall the flame kindle upon thee.

The best way to deal with fear is to recognize it for what it is and move forward. The Bible tells us that fear is not just an emotion but it can be a spirit as well.

2Timothy 1:7 For God hath not given us the spirit of fear; but of power, and of love, and of a sound mind.

Sometimes we don't move forward into our destiny, or we are not able to change because we don't know what we want. But when you know what you want and yet you are not able to break through or follow through, then what's really stopping you may be fear.

A major key to overcoming fear is to simply recognize it and storm right through it. Fear is like jet engines that can propel you in the opposite direction of your destiny. But if you just turn them around they can propel you in the correct direction or right into your life's purpose. Do something practical to overcome your fear like take a class, read a book, or do some research. I meet a lot of people who are afraid of being deceived by some false teaching or doctrine. It is good to be cautious but if we are operating in fear we might reject something new that God is trying to teach us. A good way to avoid being deceived is to get to know God's ways and character and practice hearing his voice on a regular basis.

Hebrews 5:14 But strong meat belongeth to them that are of full age, *even* those who by reason of use have their senses exercised to discern both good and evil.

If you use your gifts consistently then you will recognize what is true and what is false. This will break the strategy of fear that Satan tries to inflict to keep us from moving forward.

I used be afraid to read aloud and speak in public. Now this is what I do for a living and I love it.

Whatever we focus on continually can become our reality, whether it is rational or not. If we focus on why we cannot do something, we will never be able to do it. You might be focusing too much on how hard it is to change, instead of focusing on how easy it is to take small steps each day.

Past Wounds Rob Your Future
A major strategy that Satan uses to steal our identity is to get us to focus on our past wounds and in turn allow them to rob us of a bright future.

If you focus too much on the past you will lose your vision and begin to believe that you do not have a future.

Twenty years ago I began getting lots of deep healing in my life and growing in maturity towards my destiny.

Forgive Others

Another major strategy of Satan that will steal your identity and destiny is to get you to a place where you are not able to forgive other people when they have done something to hurt you.

Forgiveness is a key to being able to live a spiritual life full of God's love and power. We were designed by God to not hold onto anger, revenge, bitterness, and resentment. When we do, it's destructive to our being, leading to a slow and insidious breakdown of the entire system. Many people suffering from stress, anxiety, bitterness, and depression may very well need to forgive themselves and others.

The effects of bitterness and unforgiveness are not only physical but also spiritual.

Matthew 6:14 For if ye forgive men their trespasses, your heavenly Father will also forgive you:

Ephesians 4:32 And be ye kind one to another, tenderhearted, forgiving one another, even as God for Christ's sake hath forgiven you.

If you have unforgiveness you may find yourself:
- Thinking about getting revenge

- Wanting something bad to happen to a person

- Holding a grudge

- Talking about someone behind their back

- Obsessing with a memory of something someone did to you

Forgiving a person does not mean that you agree with what they did.

1. You can forgive a person, but trust may need to be rebuilt for the relationship to be restored.

2. You can also forgive a person who is no longer living.

3. You can forgive someone without telling him or her that you forgave them.

4. It is the act of forgiveness that frees things up in the spiritual realm.

5. Forgiving yourself is necessary as well. Just as unforgiveness can create negative effects—forgiving creates a positive atmosphere.

Steps to Forgiveness
List out the offenses that people have done that continue to bother you. You may have already forgiven them, but if you are still feeling the ill effects continue the process.

Go through them one by one and ask God to give you the strength to forgive them. Visually see yourself releasing the person. See the hurt you have been carrying vanish into God's light or the Cross of Christ.

If you need to, write a letter to the person or to God. You don't have to mail it. This can be expressed to a person no longer living or to someone still alive. Be honest and feel the effects this pain has had on you, not the pain itself. The goal is to let it be released from you so it no longer affects you.

Only do this if it is safe. It is not necessary to talk to a person to forgive them. Realize that forgiveness and healing is a process. It may take time. You can forgive people in your heart and spirit and benefit from the process.

As we get out of this strategy of not forgiving others we will most definitely see the benefits. It will have a positive effect on your mind and your body.

Chapter Nine
Solutions to Miracles

I have been through much physically and I tell you that there are many things we all can overcome but miracle hindrances must be broke threw. Nothing is more devastating than hearing the words, "You have cancer." It is also a frightening experience to suddenly discover that you have sugar diabetes or some other life-threatening disease.

When times such as these come, most people do not know what to do. When given such a diagnosis, many people listen to the doctor's statistics and give up, often dying prematurely. When this happens to a family member or close friend, the reaction is usually to begin preparing for the loved one's eventual death. You Don't Have to Die Prematurely.

Psalms 118:17 I shall not die, but live, and declare the works of the LORD.

We will examine what we can do to get our loved ones healed.

Spiritual Warfare
Whether we like it or not, the devil has already declared war on us. It is now up to us to learn how to fight.

Breaking of Spiritual Strongholds

Exodus 15:3 The LORD *is* a man of war: the LORD *is* his name.

God has a battle plan for His people. We can count on Him to teach us how to war if we are willing to learn. An awakening about spiritual warfare is taking place in the earth today. God is raising up warriors to go into cities and nations to pray against prevailing principalities and powers. After days of intense prayer, many major strongholds have been broken.

I went through a vicious battle with health problems. Through these experiences, I learned to war and won. It is God's will that we learn to war against sickness, just as we must against sin. We Must Locate the Enemy. We must understand that our war is against satan. As Christians begin to understand that overcoming sickness involves warfare, they will be better equipped to fight.

John 10:10 The thief cometh not, but for to steal, and to kill, and to destroy: I am come that they might have life, and that they might have *it* more abundantly.

Luke 22:31 And the Lord said, Simon, Simon, behold, Satan hath desired *to have* you, that he may sift *you* as wheat:

This shows us who our enemy is. When a person gets sick, satan taunts by saying, "There is no hope. No one ever gets healed from your disease, especially in the stage where you are. I've got you. I've got you. You're going to die."

Satan Is the Enemy of God

Satan hates humanity because he hates God and everything that is like God. When he attacks with sickness and disease, his finest weapons, his goal is to harm what God has made in His likeness.

Every time satan hurts a Christian, he hurts the heart of God, because God loves His children so much. Satan Is the Enemy of Christians Satan hates the bodies of those who are called to carry out the purposes of God. Every time he (satan) sees a human being looking and acting like God, his hatred is kindled afresh against humanity. Every time he sees a Christian, he is reminded of God, the object of his wrath. If he can attack the Christian's body, he can stop or hinder the work of God on the earth, for without a healthy body a Christian cannot live in the fullness God desires. If satan can attack a dedicated Christian's body, he can stop the attack against his kingdom. He can hinder or even stop the Christian from fulfilling the ministry God has called that Christian to do. Sometimes his attacks are counterattacks in retribution for some defeat he has experienced because of the warrior's ministry.

Sickness Is Part of the Enemy's Warfare. A good percent of Jesus' healings as recorded in the gospel of Mark involve demons. The devil also uses the natural results of the fall of humanity to cause sickness. He uses bacteria, viruses, malnutrition, accidents, fights, poison, rapists, murderers, and so forth. Regardless of the cause, the outcome of sickness is pain, suffering, and even death, which are all the works of satan.

Demons to Make People Sick

Satan has many demons whose chief business is to make people sick. When dealing with sickness, one must be aware of these various evil spirits.

Here are examples of demonic spirits that come along with cancer: the spirit of infirmity, the spirit of fear, and the spirit of bondage. Anyone who is attacked by cancer will have to battle and defeat these spirits.

Many other sicknesses are caused by spirits and must be dealt with similarly.

God's Will Concerning Sickness

Sickness and disease do not come from God. This belief alone is one of the devil's chief tricks to deceive the Church. If it was God's will for a Christian to be sick, then the Christian should not go to the doctor.

Exodus 15:26 And said, If thou wilt diligently hearken to the voice of the LORD thy God, and wilt do that which is right in his sight, and wilt give ear to his commandments, and keep all his statutes, I will put none of these diseases upon thee, which I have brought upon the Egyptians: for I *am* the LORD that healeth thee.

God's plan is for Christians to be well. In learning to War for healing, the primary purpose of this book is to teach God's people how to war for healing. When attacked by the devil, a person does not have to die. Instead, he should declare war on the sickness. Though we may not like war, we must understand that even the Kingdom of God suffers violence.

Jesus reminded us in Matthew 11:12 that from the time John the Baptist began preaching the Kingdom, the Kingdom suffered violence, and the violent took the Kingdom by force.

Matthew 11:12 And from the days of John the Baptist until now the kingdom of heaven suffereth violence, and the violent take it by force.

We wrestle against the rulers of the darkness of this world. But our war is different. The warriors are not necessarily dressed in combat boots. Sometimes they are dressed in pretty dresses and high-heel shoes.

Sometimes they are not physically strong. Sometimes they are young; sometimes they are old. But God's warriors can become mighty warriors. We do not have the same weapons that the world has, yet the weapons of our warfare are mighty through God. We wage war in a different way. We wage war by prayer. We wage war by confession. We wage war by resistance. We wage war by singing. We wage war by forgiving. We wage war by practicing gentleness. We wage war by giving up hatred and bitterness. We wage war with the truth. We wage war by feeding the hungry. We wage war by speaking in tongues. We wage war by fasting. We wage war by surrendering our wills to God. We wage war by healing the sick and in many other ways.

We have a host of angels, a heavenly Air Force that fights for us. We are the ground troops. We confront the enemy on earth in the physical realm, while our angelic cohorts confront them in the spiritual realm. We do not fight alone. We fight where we are. Sometimes we fight in the marketplace. Sometimes we fight the enemy in our homes. Sometimes we do battle with him in the hospital. But our fight is fixed. Jesus has already won the battle.

We just have to enforce it. We are developing a fighting spirit, knowing your authority, a change in mentality, visualization, goal-setting, healing words, and dealing with fear. These are the warheads that will bring destruction to the devil and release the power of healing in our bodies.

The other missiles that launch the warheads are prayer, confession, resistance, binding and loosing, preaching, testimony, breaking generational curses, and many more.

When one of God's prophets speaks concerning the healing of an individual, the sick person can war with that prophecy.

Adversaries to Healing

There are many who feel strongly that healing should not be emphasized today. There are those who argue that a study on warring for healing is not necessary. Satan, especially, will not like this study. The recommended way to deal with the enemy is to resist him.

The Bible never says that the best way to handle the devil is to ignore him. Engaging in warfare seems hard but there will be victory and is well worth the fight. The time is ripe to wipe out the deep doubt which most Christians and ministers have about disease. When a Christian is told that he has an incurable disease, this does not automatically mean he has to die. Christians do not have to accept as inevitable the many aggravating diseases that the devil puts upon them.

Chapter Ten
No to Witchcraft

A powerful revelation I found was that witchcraft cannot be released against the obedient. When a person walks in obedience to God, witchcraft has no power over him. Satan is confined to darkness, so he has no access to us when we are joined with God, in whom is no darkness at all.

Jude 1:6 And the angels which kept not their first estate, but left their own habitation, he hath reserved in everlasting chains under darkness unto the judgment of the great day.

1John 1:5 This then is the message which we have heard of him, and declare unto you, that God is light, and in him is no darkness at all.

The effects of witchcraft are obvious in our society. Though subtle, they are no less real in the church. This teaching will address when a believer is protected against witchcraft—and when he is not!

Blessing Not a Curse

During their wilderness journey the children of Israel camped on the plains of Moab. They had just attacked and defeated Bashan. Earlier they had destroyed the Amorites because they would not allow the Israelites to pass through their territory.

Now as they camped in the midst of Moab, Balak, the king of Moab and Midian, was worried. His kingdom quaked in fear at the multitude of Israelites. They knew Israel had destroyed every nation that opposed them. So King Balak sent word to the prophet Balaam. Balaam was renowned for his spiritual accuracy and insight. The king knew what-ever Balaam prophesied happened. If he blessed, they were blessed; if he cursed, they were cursed. After receiving two sets of ambassadors, Balaam consented to accompany the king to see if he could curse the children of Israel. He had been won over by the king's offer of money and honor. But Balaam warned the king that he was restricted to speak only the words God placed in his mouth. The next day they climbed the high places of Baal so Balaam could observe the nation of Israel. After Balaam had assessed them, he instructed the king to erect seven altars and prepare sacrifices for each of them. Then Balaam opened his mouth to curse Israel, but instead he pronounced a blessing over them. Needless to say the king was very upset.

Numbers 23:11 And Balak said unto Balaam, What hast thou done unto me? I took thee to curse mine enemies, and, behold, thou hast blessed *them* altogether.

So Balaam suggested they move to a higher level in the hope of giving Balak what he wanted. Again they erected seven altars and offered additional sacrifices. But when Balaam opened his mouth he again blessed Israel instead of cursing them.

This entire process was repeated two more times. Each time Balaam attempted to curse but was compelled by God to bless Israel. In Balaam's second oracle we find this profound statement:

He has not observed iniquity in Jacob, Nor has He seen wickedness in Israel. The Lord his God is with him, And the shout of a King is among them. God brings them out of Egypt; He has strength like a wild ox. For there is no sorcery against Jacob, Nor any divination against Israel.

Numbers 23:21-23 He hath not beheld iniquity in Jacob, neither hath he seen perverseness in Israel: the LORD his God *is* with him, and the shout of a king *is* among them. God brought them out of Egypt; he hath as it were the strength of an unicorn. Surely *there is* no enchantment against Jacob, neither *is there* any divination against Israel: according to this time it shall be said of Jacob and of Israel, What hath God wrought!

Israel walked in covenant with God. His mighty arm had delivered them from Egyptian oppression, symbolizing freedom from this world system and power. They were a forgiven and cleansed nation, baptized as they passed through the Red Sea.

God said He observed no iniquity in them. Balaam declared that because of Israel's covenant with God there was no sorcery or divination that could prosper against them. You could also state the principle this way: There is no witchcraft that works against God's people, nor any divination against His church!

We should encourage ourselves with this promise. Let the witches and warlocks rant, rave, and burn their candles. Let them recite their hexes, spells, and curses—not one can harm a child of God!

They will not prevail against the church of the living God.

Proverbs 26:2 As the bird by wandering, as the swallow by flying, so the curse causeless shall not come.

Numbers 23:8 How shall I curse, whom God hath not cursed? or how shall I defy, *whom* the LORD hath not defied?

Hide me from the secret plots of the wicked, From the rebellion of the workers of iniquity, Who sharpen their tongue like a sword, And bend their bows to shoot their arrows—bitter words, That they may shoot in secret at the blameless.

Psalms 64:2-4 Hide me from the secret counsel of the wicked; from the insurrection of the workers of iniquity: Who whet their tongue like a sword, *and* bend *their bows to shoot* their arrows, *even* bitter words: That they may shoot in secret at the perfect: suddenly do they shoot at him, and fear not.

Curses may be released against the righteous, but they will not rest upon him. Watch what happens to those who release curses:

Psalms 64:7, 8 But God shall shoot at them *with* an arrow; suddenly shall they be wounded. So they shall make their own tongue to fall upon themselves: all that see them shall flee away.

Notice they stumble over their own tongue. The very words they release to hurt others will circle back upon them. In another metaphor David explained it this way.

Psalms 57:6 They have prepared a net for my steps; my soul is bowed down: they have digged a pit before me, into the midst whereof they are fallen *themselves*. Selah.

Even if Balaam had pronounced curses over the children of Israel, it only would have returned upon his own head. Balaam knew it was impossible to bring a witchcraft curse on God's people, even though he wanted to. Moses later reminded Israel,

Deuteronomy 23:4, 5 Because they met you not with bread and with water in the way, when ye came forth out of Egypt; and because they hired against thee Balaam the son of Beor of Pethor of Mesopotamia, to curse thee. Nevertheless the LORD thy God would not hearken unto Balaam; but the LORD thy God turned the curse into a blessing unto thee, because the LORD thy God loved thee.

Numbers 24:10, 11 And Balak's anger was kindled against Balaam, and he smote his hands together: and Balak said unto Balaam, I called thee to curse mine enemies, and, behold, thou hast altogether blessed *them* these three times. Therefore now flee thou to thy place: I thought to promote thee unto great honour; but, lo, the LORD hath kept thee back from honour.

The king was planning to give Balaam a great monetary reward and honor for cursing his enemies. But in essence the king told Balaam, "You can forget the reward. Your God obviously doesn't want you to have it. So get out of my sight."

Balaam and Balak, we read an amazing thing.

Numbers 25:1-2 And Israel abode in Shittim, and the people began to commit whoredom with the daughters of Moab. And they called the people unto the sacrifices of their gods: and the people did eat, and bowed down to their gods. And Israel joined himself unto Baalpeor: and the anger of the LORD was kindled against Israel.

What happened to this nation that had served the Lord? The Book of Revelation says that Balaam,

Revelations 2:14 But I have a few things against thee, because thou hast there them that hold the doctrine of Balaam, who taught Balac to cast a stumblingblock before the children of Israel, to eat things sacrificed unto idols, and to commit fornication.

Numbers 31:16 Behold, these caused the children of Israel, through the counsel of Balaam, to commit trespass against the LORD in the matter of Peor, and there was a plague among the congregation of the LORD.

I can just picture the scene. Balaam really wanted the king's money. So he said to the king, "I can't curse them with my mouth or any other form of divination, but I can tell you how to get them under a witchcraft curse!" King Balak said, "How can it be done?" Balaam said, "Send your women and have them infiltrate Israel's camp. Have them bring their idols with them as well. This rebellion will bring them under a witchcraft curse."

Israel's disobedience caused a nation that could not be cursed to come under a severe plague.

Numbers 25:3 And Israel joined himself unto Baalpeor: and the anger of the LORD was kindled against Israel.

Numbers 25:9 And those that died in the plague were twenty and four thousand.

This was the greatest single loss Israel experienced in the wilderness, and it was all a result of their rebellion. Radical disobedience opened the door to a radical plague. Their rebellion was so blatant that one Israelite man openly flaunted his sin with a Midianite woman in the sight of Moses and the entire congregation of Israel.

So what stopped the plague? You may have guessed—radical obedience!

Numbers 25:7, 8 And when Phinehas, the son of Eleazar, the son of Aaron the priest, saw *it,* he rose up from among the congregation, and took a javelin in his hand; And he went after the man of Israel into the tent, and thrust both of them through, the man of Israel, and the woman through her belly. So the plague was stayed from the children of Israel.

Allow me to point out that God is not the author of plagues and diseases. The children of Israel had blatantly rebelled and breached His covering of protection. The door was opened, so the enemy came in with his curse. Once again this affirms that rebellion is witchcraft. It gives legal entrance to Satan's control. Israel escaped the curse of a soothsayer only to be decimated by its own disobedience.

The apostle Paul wrote a stern letter to the Galatians.

Galatians 1:2 And all the brethren which are with me, unto the churches of Galatia:

Notice this letter was addressed to the churches, not the general populace of Galatia. Paul chided:

Galatians 3:1 O foolish Galatians, who hath bewitched you, that ye should not obey the truth, before whose eyes Jesus Christ hath been evidently set forth, crucified among you?

God had revealed His salvation by grace to these churches by Paul's preaching. But it was not long before they began to disobey what once was clear to them. They turned to follow another gospel one of works

Galatians 3:16 Now to Abraham and his seed were the promises made. He saith not, And to seeds, as of many; but as of one, And to thy seed, which is Christ.

However, this specific act of disobedience is not what I want to focus on. What is important is the fact that God had clearly revealed His will to them, and they turned from it to follow the reasoning of another. This reasoning bewitched them to the point of confusion. Paul warned this church that they were under the influence of witchcraft. Some may question, "I thought there was no divination or witchcraft against God's people?"

That is correct; no curse can be released against the obedient. But remember, rebellion or disobedience places a person under witchcraft.

Now let me make this point clear. We come under bewitchment when we disobey what God has made clear to us—not when we disobey what has not been revealed to us. What they disobeyed had been clearly revealed to the Galatians.

Chapter Eleven
Learning Obedience God's Way

Some may be surprised that for us to learn obedience it may be the Hard Way. We need to learn this to see Breakthrough of Spiritual Strongholds. We are going to see the open doors that come from being obedient. Repentance is the key when we do this God's way. Most importantly we will understand the tragic consequences of disobedience.

I have met many in the church who live in disobedience. Their lives consist of one crisis after another. There is always some problem they just can't seem to get victory in. They escape one to find themselves in another. Each scenario seems to become progressively worse. These problems consume their time, energy, and livelihood. I have watched while their marriages end in divorce. They are passed over for promotions or, worse, even lose their jobs. They fall victim to theft, financial crisis, and tragedy.

Frustrated, they frantically look for someone to blame—it is the fault of their husband, wife, parent, pastor, boss, government, or any other. Yet the truth is this: somewhere a door stands open, making them vulnerable to an onslaught of demonic oppression and attack. There are two culprits at work that actually feed off each other. The first is deception. This darkness is found in their hearts because they have not obeyed God's Word.

James 1:22 But be ye doers of the word, and not hearers only, deceiving your own selves.

The second culprit is the tangled snare of controlling spirits who are sanctioned to attack at will because of disobedience. The paradox: because the people are deceived, they blame everything except their own disobedience. This blinds them to exactly what is needed to secure their freedom.

Thank God for His Word. Its light exposes deception by discerning the thoughts and intentions of our hearts.

Hebrews 4:12 For the word of God *is* quick, and powerful, and sharper than any twoedged sword, piercing even to the dividing asunder of soul and spirit, and of the joints and marrow, and *is* a discerner of the thoughts and intents of the heart.

David said it this way,

Psalms 119:67 Before I was afflicted I went astray: but now have I kept thy word.

Psalms 119:71 *It is* good for me that I have been afflicted; that I might learn thy statutes.

Unfortunately, when some are afflicted due to disobedience they refuse to learn. They continue wandering in the wilderness of disobedience. They blame everyone else instead of learning from their error. I must stop here to clarify a point. Every time a person faces difficulty, problems, or hardships it is not necessarily the product of disobedience. It is a fact that many suffer while in obedience to God.

Joseph was just such a man. He was not disobedient. Yet he spent years in slavery even though he was born free. Then he spent over two years in Pharaoh's dungeon—not as a result of disobedience but as the result of obedience to God. He fled sexual immorality, shunning seduction. Obedience increased his hardship. But even as he suffered, men could still perceive God's favor on his life. It was evidenced by Joseph's godly fear and obedience.

Genesis 39:2, 3 And the LORD was with Joseph, and he was a prosperous man; and he was in the house of his master the Egyptian. And his master saw that the LORD *was* with him, and that the LORD made all that he did to prosper in his hand.

Genesis 39:21-23 But the LORD was with Joseph, and shewed him mercy, and gave him favour in the sight of the keeper of the prison. And the keeper of the prison committed to Joseph's hand all the prisoners that *were* in the prison; and whatsoever they did there, he was the doer *of it*. The keeper of the prison looked not to any thing *that was* under his hand; because the LORD was with him, and *that* which he did, the LORD made *it* to prosper.

Cain also suffered but for a totally different reason. Offended, he refused to repent of his disobedience. This resulted in a curse over his life. He lived his years on the earth as a fugitive and a vagabond. His aimless and hopeless wanderings were an example to the generations that followed him. It was a warning of the price of refusal to repent and obey God.

The Blessing Comes After Obedience

There is great blessing when a person truly repents of disobedience. Joel cried,

Joel 2:13, 14 And rend your heart, and not your garments, and turn unto the LORD your God: for he *is* gracious and merciful, slow to anger, and of great kindness, and repenteth him of the evil. Who knoweth *if* he will return and repent, and leave a blessing behind him; *even* a meat offering and a drink offering unto the LORD your God?

It has not only been good for us but also for the kingdom. It is the blessing of obedience.

Obedience Is the Key

Our thoughts in life, as "fallen people," have caused wars, fights, strife, gossip, discord, pain, and everything else that is evil and negative in the world. We must read, pray, worship, and praise God every chance we get. Doing these things is how I have overcome with the help of the Holy Spirit, whom I have learned to love so much. Show Him that you love Him with every thing you have in your heart. Thank Him always because He is so good. He will help you to worship when you don't know how or are having trouble doing so. Just keep reaching the heart of your Father, and He will help you learn to deal with the issues that come your way. This is an everyday process.

It is not over until you are gone to Heaven or the rapture takes place. Jesus is your friend when you need Him to be, and I'm confident you desire that kind of friendship.

This is a sign of loving Him: adore His commandments and obey; read His Word, meditating on it night and day, regardless of whether you feel like it or not.

1John 5:3 For this is the love of God, that we keep his commandments: and his commandments are not grievous.

Learn to call to Him, "Hosanna!" when things are falling apart and you do not have any money in your bank account to pay for anything. Run to Him in your troubles, and run to Him when things are good. If you remain in Him, you will do well and accomplish many things.

In the past, relatives and believers in the Body of Christ have challenged me negatively and given me wrong information, but I learned to forgive and love every one of them, regardless of what they have done. Forgiveness is such a *huge* factor in the Church. Trials and tests that come through other people can become wearying and hectic to new believers, who must rely on the Lord for guidance and courage. He is always with us.

Hebrews 13:5 *Let your* conversation *be* without covetousness; *and be* content with such things as ye have: for he hath said, I will never leave thee, nor forsake thee.

1Samuel 15:22 And Samuel said, Hath the LORD *as great* delight in burnt offerings and sacrifices, as in obeying the voice of the LORD? Behold, to obey *is* better than sacrifice, *and* to hearken than the fat of rams.

1John 5:3 For this is the love of God, that we keep his commandments: and his commandments are not grievous.

Chapter Twelve
Cast All Your Cares

For you too really see the full breakthrough, we must Cast All Your Cares to Christ. Even though some may see God's love as weakness, they have to realize that He will only endure so much before His judgment falls on them.

This is why He has given us the manuscript to walk in His statutes and will. His mercy endures forever; this is one reason why my soul cries out to God.

1Chronicles 16:34 O give thanks unto the LORD; for *he is* good; for his mercy *endureth* for ever.

His goodness is so wonderful and impeccable, not just because He is a giver of all things. I have learned to love Him and recognize His goodness regardless of whether I am living in plenty or in want. We must take that into consideration without complaining and murmuring.

Philippians 2:14 Do all things without murmurings and disputings:

We must learn to cast our cares upon the Lord because He really does care about us.

1Peter 5:7 Casting all your care upon him; for he careth for you.

Psalms 55:22 Cast thy burden upon the LORD, and he shall sustain thee: he shall never suffer the righteous to be moved.

When we cast our cares on Him, no matter what the issue is, we must not take it back by worrying. This is how we take it back—by constantly speaking about it and holding on to it even after we have released it. God is greater than we can ever imagine. Worry is the absence of hope and faith. Always asking questions about how God is going to take care of our problems is also a type of "taking it back." If we continue to worry in this manner, it's a sign of doubt. He will never leave us, though on occasion it may feel like He's not around.

James 1:5-8 If any of you lack wisdom, let him ask of God, that giveth to all *men* liberally, and upbraideth not; and it shall be given him. But let him ask in faith, nothing wavering. For he that wavereth is like a wave of the sea driven with the wind and tossed. For let not that man think that he shall receive any thing of the Lord. A double minded man *is* unstable in all his ways.

Let your conduct be without covetousness; be content with such things as you have.

Hebrews 13:5 *Let your* conversation *be* without covetousness; *and be* content with such things as ye have: for he hath said, I will never leave thee, nor forsake thee.

Integrity

There are many examples of rejection-fueled behavior and lack of integrity in the Body of Christ. This may seem or feel insignificant, but many people have left churches because no one would talk to them or say hello. It does affect the heart of the Image-Bearer (Christian). When individuals act with a lack of integrity on a constant basis, it tells me a lot about them.

If I am always reaching out, but no one reaches back, that behavior is called a lack of integrity. Certainly it is not always a sign of, "I really don't care," or an "out of sight, out of mind" philosophy. I can see past the artificial attitude and the church face of a synthetic spirit. The Lord doesn't agree with this kind of behavior. We all serve the same God, so we must treat each other like we matter.

We must be men and women of our word. If we say we are going to do something, we must do just that. If we are not able to act upon our word, then we should let the person know.

I have had many Christians come to me after Church and say let's go out to eat and they would say "I'll buy". We would go to the restaurant and when it was time for the checks they would say "two checks please." It got me to a place that after it happen I wouldn't go out because of past experiences.

Jesus wants us to be a community of people who hold on to our words. We all have our days of not being able to carry out what we say, and that's OK at times, but integrity is very important in the Body of Christ. We cannot say something and not mean it. We must go forward with keeping our appointments and obligations without deviating as much as possible. And when we cannot fulfill our commitment or make the appointment, we must be courteous enough to call and inform people. Here's another example.

Say a man has a son from a previous relationship; the child is anxious, excited, and ready to spend time with his father, but the father ends up not showing up. Not only will the boy be deeply hurt (especially if this is a repeated occurrence), but it will not be long before he stops believing his father. This can generate contention between the child and father as well as between the separated mother and father. This kind of thinking and irresponsibility can bring problems into a person's life as a whole, if not dealt with quickly.

Here's what the Bible says about the importance of integrity:

Proverbs 20:7 The just *man* walketh in his integrity: his children *are* blessed after him.

Proverbs 19:1 Better *is* the poor that walketh in his integrity, than *he that is* perverse in his lips, and is a fool.

Proverbs 11:3 The integrity of the upright shall guide them: but the perverseness of transgressors shall destroy them.

Psalms 78:72 So he fed them according to the integrity of his heart; and guided them by the skilfulness of his hands.

Psalms 26:1 *A Psalm* of David. Judge me, O LORD; for I have walked in mine integrity: I have trusted also in the LORD; *therefore* I shall not slide.

The Mind of God

According to our standards, we think we know better than God when it comes to knowing what would be best for us. When God calls us to His ministry, the pursuit begins.

He's trying to get something to us, not take from us. There are many Scripture passages that prove His wisdom.

Proverbs 2:1-9 My son, if thou wilt receive my words, and hide my commandments with thee; So that thou incline thine ear unto wisdom, *and* apply thine heart to understanding; Yea, if thou criest after knowledge, *and* liftest up thy voice for understanding; If thou seekest her as silver, and searchest for her as *for* hid treasures; Then shalt thou understand the fear of the LORD, and find the knowledge of God. For the LORD giveth wisdom: out of his mouth *cometh* knowledge and understanding. He layeth up sound wisdom for the righteous: *he is* a buckler to them that walk uprightly. He keepeth the paths of judgment, and preserveth the way of his saints. Then shalt thou understand righteousness, and judgment, and equity; *yea,* every good path.

His mind is beyond human comprehension.

However, He has given us His Spirit to help us understand just enough of His intelligence so that we can partake of it and come into a more profound understanding.

Before your brokenness period visits you, pray always, especially for God to give you the strength, grace, and power of the Holy Ghost to go through it and endure.

Psalms 23:4 Yea, though I walk through the valley of the shadow of death, I will fear no evil: for thou *art* with me; thy rod and thy staff they comfort me.

Romans 8:27 And he that searcheth the hearts knoweth what *is* the mind of the Spirit, because he maketh intercession for the saints according to *the will of* God.

Romans 8:34 Who *is* he that condemneth? *It is* Christ that died, yea rather, that is risen again, who is even at the right hand of God, who also maketh intercession for us.

You are *never* alone! It is awesome to hear, "I am going through something right now." Operative word, *through*. Praise the Lord you are going through, rather then staying and wallowing in it. Keep this in the center of your thoughts, "This too shall pass."

It's Always Worth It

You will be like gold when He is done with you. "Ready and willing" will become your motto. People will start to notice a change in your life and character. In the end, it will be wonderful to see and experience. When you look back at your life, you will say, "I cannot believe I went through that. I endured, and I am still here." You will be better than before, much closer to the likeness of Christ. It won't be you, but God Himself who assists you to be a man or woman of humility. And in this humility, you will be able to stand and receive correction, and others will sense that you are approachable and easier to talk to.

Once you have allowed brokenness to come, He can pour out the sweet-smelling oil of anointing on your spirit. Your heart of stone conforms into the heart of flesh that Christ would desire. The Holy Spirit can do His will easier, without any additional obstacles against Him. You will be able to listen to God and hear others more clearly. The Lord is able to speak to you and guide you. Communication with people will become easier as your meekness gives God glory. Meekness is power under control.

Father God

I received a prophetic Word that said "I the Lord will be to you the Father that you need." My life was changed from that day forward. God wants to do the same for you. Speaking about meekness and being lowly was a very long process for me. I have cried and yelled with ceaseless tears to get where I am today.

The pain and suffering I had to bear were agonizing and extremely lonely. I experienced betrayals, loneliness, let downs, beatings, bullying, my own foolishness, misery, lack of love, problems I created for myself, accusations, being abused and being homeless like experiences with my mother for almost a year in the streets of a city where I knew no one. It caused me to build a huge wall in my heart to prevent anyone from penetrating it and seeing the person I really was. Periodically, my father would show up in my life. I can remember my dad died when I was six and my mother had a lot of health problems.

Being homeless caused everything to be stripped from me. I was walking and wondering every day where God was in all of this, and where my natural father was. In my heart of hearts, I had to start all over again from scratch since I was stripped until nothing remained.

In many ways, this broke me, and yet I was hard-hearted like Pharaoh.

Exodus 7:13 And he hardened Pharaoh's heart, that he hearkened not unto them; as the LORD had said.

All of my life has been one huge trial without me seeing or experiencing an oasis. People in the world, my friends, and my family didn't understand me. All along, there was a call on my life, and I didn't even know it. At the same time, I was feeling the four walls of loneliness close in on me. I wondered *where my Dad in Heaven is.* Eventually, the Lord did show up.

When I received that word later in my life, that Jesus was visiting me when I was a young child, it made a great amount of sense. My Father God, after all, has been there through all the hell I had to experience. The spiritual ingredient to all of this was to forgive my parents, God, and most importantly, myself.

Protecting the Anointing

Have you ever had anyone come into your circle of friends who never went through hell, like you have, but who tried to preach to you or tell you what to do?

Luke 7:47 Wherefore I say unto thee, Her sins, which are many, are forgiven; for she loved much: but to whom little is forgiven, *the same* loveth little.

When you love the Lord much it's because He has forgiven you for so many things you have done wrong in your life. In return, you desire to love the Lord with everything you've got!

However, certain Believers haven't even touched the surface of your past sufferings to understand you enough but yet they desire to teach you how to overcome your situation. Plus, they may not love their God as much as you do. My question is: So what can such people teach us? How are they able to minister to us when all they have gone through is not being able to put gas in their cars or having a hard time trying to park closer to the stores entrance?

What has God really delivered them from? People who have experienced real hell in their lives will give Jesus all the glory and honor for fixing their mess, thanking Him daily for saving them. Not to try to state (whether a friend or associate) will bend over backward for the Lord, or you, when you can see clearly past their agenda. This goes to show we must be very meticulous about who we allow to take part in our lives. Some may seem they are after our best interests at first, when in turn they are insensitive, conniving, having other plans to hurt you. It may not be physical; a person can hurt you spiritually as well. We must walk vigilantly and caution ourselves against spiritual leeches; they will suck us dry until every ounce of energy is absorbed. Some believers would cling to us because they realize who we are in the Spirit and the gift that has been bestowed upon our lives. They make it their goal to leech from the anointing, wanting the easy way.

We must be cautious of those who want what we have and who try to drain us every chance they get. They want to steal, kill, and destroy what God has implanted deep down inside of us—pulling on us, fishing and trying to get to know our character and motives. We must stay away from the artificial and counterfeit Christians who are trying to consume us in the spirit!

My boldness is necessary, but this is one of the reasons why I wrote about this topic. It's dangerous in these evil times. I know some will not go through all this just to have the anointing, but I was trying to prove a point.

Again, to make my point clear, we must not allow just anyone to come into our lives with harmful agendas with what God has instilled in us just because they said God told them to be part of our lives. We must be careful in these perilous times.

2Timothy 3:1-5 This know also, that in the last days perilous times shall come. For men shall be lovers of their own selves, covetous, boasters, proud, blasphemers, disobedient to parents, unthankful, unholy, Without natural affection, trucebreakers, false accusers, incontinent, fierce, despisers of those that are good, Traitors, heady, highminded, lovers of pleasures more than lovers of God; Having a form of godliness, but denying the power thereof: from such turn away.

Pride

Rather you know it or not if you have pride it can be nearly impossible to see Breakthrough of Spiritual Strongholds. When people walk in the spirit of pride, we can discern the spirit simply by being around them because the Holy Spirit tells us. If we're not sure, we can just pay close attention to what kind of tree they are and the fruit they produce. Some fruit has worms in the center, so we must be very careful.

Proverbs 16:18, 19 Pride *goeth* before destruction, and an haughty spirit before a fall. Better *it is to be* of an humble spirit with the lowly, than to divide the spoil with the proud.

Proverbs 13:10 Only by pride cometh contention: but with the well advised *is* wisdom.

Jesus was tempted by the devil with a question associated with the "pride of life." As I have studied the Word of the Lord, I came to know Him on a deeper, more intimate level. I see what pride and its spiritual cousins (arrogance, conceit, pleasure, self-gratification, and smugness) were doing to me and in all of my relationships. Before I began to perceive my "Valley of Brokenness," I had to step into my own life first to see what others saw in me, with the help of the Spirit of God. He helped me to see all the junk that was killing me on the inside, which I did not discern before. If we do not draw near to God so God can draw near to us, it will suffocate our relationships with others, too. Having vision is not the same as having sight, and this is part of being Kingdom-minded, which I will write about later.

Ending Cycles of Pain

As we learn how to be vigilant and sober in the things of the spirit that come our way, especially related to the vision of our leaders, God will take us to different heights in the Spirit that will bring us to our knees. We will have no other choice but to fight satan and his minions with the Word of God. When believers in Christ come against this celebrated idea, that the enemy thinks he has us cornered, this is when strong opposition by prayer will start on the part of the Believer.

Luke 4:5-8 And the devil, taking him up into an high mountain, shewed unto him all the kingdoms of the world in a moment of time. And the devil said unto him, All this power will I give thee, and the glory of them: for that is delivered unto me; and to whomsoever I will I give it. If thou therefore wilt worship me, all shall be thine. And Jesus answered and said unto him, Get thee behind me, Satan: for it is written, Thou shalt worship the Lord thy God, and him only shalt thou serve.

Imagine how I would look stealing a brand new television out of someone's home and then trying to sell it back to them? It's absolutely foolish. The devil offered to Jesus the kingdoms, cities, people, houses, and such—which *already belonged to Jesus*—knowing in his mind that Jesus already owned them. Jesus would not bow down to satan; He recognized his pride and self-centered desires of sinfulness and wickedness.

Matthew 4:8-11 Again, the devil taketh him up into an exceeding high mountain, and sheweth him all the kingdoms of the world, and the glory of them; And saith unto him, All these things will I give thee, if thou wilt fall down and worship me. Then saith Jesus unto him, Get thee hence, Satan: for it is written, Thou shalt worship the Lord thy God, and him only shalt thou serve. Then the devil leaveth him, and, behold, angels came and ministered unto him.

Pride is all about *me* and what *I* can get out of the deal. Pride destroys without the concern of others. Self-gratification in all areas of life is satan's evil fill. Caution should be our middle name because pride is a spirit of leviathan. Beware of that spirit; it will eradicate anyone, saved or unsaved. In the end, we know God Almighty will punish that spirit.

Isaiah 27:1 In that day the LORD with his sore and great and strong sword shall punish leviathan the piercing serpent, even leviathan that crooked serpent; and he shall slay the dragon that *is* in the sea.

Psalms 74:14 Thou brakest the heads of leviathan in pieces, *and* gavest him *to be* meat to the people inhabiting the wilderness.

Self-importance and smugness always take from others and are constantly greedy for more. Those with these attitudes are never satisfied with the now. Impatience is the cousin of pride. If we are not aware and on guard; these spirits will creep in and tear down what we hold dear.

Ephesians 4:26 Be ye angry, and sin not: let not the sun go down upon your wrath:

James 1:4 But let patience have *her* perfect work, that ye may be perfect and entire, wanting nothing.

Ending Cycles of Pain

Song of Solomon 2:15 Take us the foxes, the little foxes, that spoil the vines: for our vines *have* tender grapes.

Sometimes we try to look for the big things to see what a person deals with, when in reality, we must never lose focus to the little foxes which are the little problems that may arise discreetly causing you to lose focus on God's promises for your life. We have to be careful and wise in the Spirit, letting God help us to be more like Him and to break the spirit of pride off of our lives.

Now that I have learned to be patient, I know now being patient was a very important part of my brokenness that was necessary for change.

In the past, humility was not my strong point. There were times when pride came and raised its ugly head, and I had to fight against myself with the power of the Spirit. Keeping this ugly spirit as far away from me as possible helps me to see clearly. Pride doesn't like anyone telling it what to do.

People who are walking in pride feel like they do not need any help because they have everything under control and figured out. We must be aware that pride can bring other spirits into our lives if we don't deal with it immediately. We need to realize that we deal with things that are in "high places"

Ephesians 6:12 For we wrestle not against flesh and blood, but against principalities, against powers, against the rulers of the darkness of this world, against spiritual wickedness in high *places*.

The truth is, words hurt, destroying the lives of people by the thousands. If only graves could speak. As we read Scripture, encounter the parable about the prodigal son.

Luke 15:11-32 And he said, A certain man had two sons: And the younger of them said to *his* father, Father, give me the portion of goods that falleth *to me*. And he divided unto them *his* living. And not many days after the younger son gathered all together, and took his journey into a far country, and there wasted his substance with riotous living. And when he had spent all, there arose a mighty famine in that land; and he began to be in want. And he went and joined himself to a citizen of that country; and he sent him into his fields to feed swine. And he would fain have filled his belly with the husks that the swine did eat: and no man gave unto him. And when he came to himself, he said, How many hired servants of my father's have bread enough and to spare, and I perish with hunger! I will arise and go to my father, and will say unto him, Father, I have sinned against heaven, and before thee, And am no more worthy to be called thy son: make me as one of thy hired servants. And he arose, and came to his father. But when he was yet a great way off, his father saw him, and had compassion, and ran, and fell on his neck, and kissed him. And the son said unto him, Father, I have sinned against heaven, and in thy sight, and am no more worthy to be called thy son. But the father said to his servants, Bring forth the best robe, and put *it* on him; and put a ring on his hand, and shoes on *his* feet: And bring hither the fatted calf, and kill *it;* and let us eat, and be merry: For this my son was dead, and is alive again; he was lost, and is found. And they began to be merry. Now his elder son was in the field: and as he came and drew nigh to the house, he heard musick and dancing. And he called one of the servants, and asked what these things meant. And he said unto him, Thy brother is come; and thy father hath killed the fatted calf, because he hath received him safe and sound. And he was angry, and would not go in: therefore came his father out, and intreated him. And he answering said to *his* father, Lo, these many years do I serve thee, neither transgressed I at any time thy commandment: and yet thou never gavest me a kid, that I might make merry with my friends: But as soon as this thy son was come, which hath devoured thy living with harlots, thou hast killed for him the fatted calf. And he said unto him, Son, thou art ever with me, and all that I have is thine. It was meet that we should make merry, and be glad: for this thy brother was dead, and is alive again; and was lost, and is found.

1Peter 3:8-12 Finally, *be ye* all of one mind, having compassion one of another, love as brethren, *be* pitiful, *be* courteous: Not rendering evil for evil, or railing for railing: but contrariwise blessing; knowing that ye are thereunto called, that ye should inherit a blessing. For he that will love life, and see good days, let him refrain his tongue from evil, and his lips that they speak no guile: Let him eschew evil, and do good; let him seek peace, and ensue it. For the eyes of the Lord *are* over the righteous, and his ears *are open* unto their prayers: but the face of the Lord *is* against them that do evil.

Renewed and Accepted

No matter the concern or need, the Holy Spirit will run to your rescue. Being able to praise God with my whole heart feels so good; I am no longer in bondage to those things. Everyday I wake up by the grace of God and start my day refreshed and renewed, never looking back or returning to that man I once was.

Admitting that I sinned against my own family and friends has helped me appreciate and realize new mercies in Christ. I would not even blame them if they did not forgive me, but I praise God that they did. I had to know myself all over again, and the Holy Ghost came and filled me (and He still is filling me to this day). Thank you, Jesus!

After the change in me, old friends from the past would still come up to me and try to incite the old me. The cool thing is, I didn't have to give them Bible passages, plead the blood, or give them an entire church program explaining how I had changed for the better. Just something simple would be sufficient.

When the Lord does a perfect work in us, we will have the enemy bring people up from our past to rekindle the *old person*. We must not hesitate to say that the *old person* no longer exists. We will thank ourselves later for the trouble we have avoided, and we will bring glory to God! We should never take away His glory for the change in our lives; He deserves every single word of praise for it.

Chapter Thirteen
Our Spiritual Identity

This is one of the most powerful Spiritual battles that need Breakthrough. Throughout the Bible we see God's plan for people unfold. In the Garden of Eden God was in direct relationship with Adam and Eve. He walked in the garden with them and allowed them to eat from the tree of life that was the source of their immortality. In this garden paradise there was also the tree of the knowledge of good and evil and God had told them not to eat the fruit of that tree or they would die (lose their immortality).

The serpent (Satan) got them to believe that if they ate the fruit of the tree of knowledge of good and evil their eyes would be opened and they would be like God, knowing good and evil. As they found out, Satan was lying to them and they were robbed of their true spiritual identity. The two trees in the garden represent the two sources of spirituality or spiritual identity. The tree of life is the spiritual source that is pure and from God and now awaits us in Heaven. The second is the tree of the knowledge of good and evil.

God's original intention for us was to only know and experience pure life in a world that had no sickness or death.

1John 4:8 He that loveth not knoweth not God; for God is love.

The tree of knowledge of good and evil has a mixture of good intentions, yet the possibility of evil results. The good news is that we have been restored in our spiritual relationship with God through Jesus Christ.

I do want to remind people that as I reveal these strategies of Satan to destroy us, God is much more powerful and desires to bring an amazing amount of acceptance, love, and unlimited power into our lives. You can have a close relationship with God as was originally intended. However, we will still battle with the fact that we also have the temptation and pull by Satan to live our life and use our gifts in a mixture of "good and evil."

Satan helped open the possibilities of "good and evil" into the world. We no longer have just pure life and love, but now we can have good intentions that can get tweaked or distorted. An example is that you can have wealth and use your money to help people in need. Then again, people with great wealth can be tempted with greed and power that will result in being unjust and ripping people off.

We are all given gifts from God—some from birth. Some of these gifts lie dormant until we are spiritually awakened (or born again) and we invite the Holy Spirit into our life. We are all born with an amazing potential to fulfill the highest destiny and purpose in God, yet we drop down to what we think we can do.

God's love and power have no limits and what we can accomplish with His Holy Spirit working through us has no limits either.

Spiritual identity theft occurs when Satan tries to get you to think that you don't have these gifts and potential and that you have no clear destiny. I have found after working with hundreds of people through healing and deliverance that the areas of your life where you are experiencing the most attack or resistance may very well be an indicator of what some of your gifts and callings are. Why would Satan waste time attacking you if you did not have a great destiny to fulfill?

I now help people who are stuck and not able to move forward in their lives. I also have discovered that there are many dreams that we can have at night that point toward our life dreams. There is a viewpoint held by some Christians that if we can avoid sin at all costs and become holy, then we will have a close relationship with God. Though there is truth in this, it has its downside. We can become so focused on avoiding sin that it becomes all we think about. Then Satan comes along and brings the mixture of evil to our good efforts. If we are spending a lot of effort on being holy then there is a chance that we feel guilty and condemned when we have areas of our life that have not been worked out yet.

The Holy Spirit will convict us of our sin but Satan tries to condemn us, causing us to feel separated from God when we sin. A better approach to holiness is getting into a close relationship with God by placing our focus on His goodness and love for us. Yes, repent when you fall short, but if you put your energy toward doing well and loving others instead of avoiding sin you will find yourself sinning less.

This is a strategy of Satan to steal away our most basic and profound identity that we are sons and daughters of God and can have a relationship with Him that is not based on rules but on the Father's great love and the Son's great sacrifice for us. I am going to reveal several strategies that Satan will attempt to use against us and I'll provide several remedies as well. This is not intended to inflict fear or to get you to focus too much on the attacks of Satan. It is simply meant to bring these plans into the light so you can put a plan of action in place and go for all that God has for you in your life.

Missing Your Destiny

Here is a good example of someone missing their destiny.

Luke 18:18-25 And a certain ruler asked him, saying, Good Master, what shall I do to inherit eternal life? And Jesus said unto him, Why callest thou me good? none *is* good, save one, *that is,* God. Thou knowest the commandments, Do not commit adultery, Do not kill, Do not steal, Do not bear false witness, Honour thy father and thy mother. And he said, All these have I kept from my youth up. Now when Jesus heard these things, he said unto him, Yet lackest thou one thing: sell all that thou hast, and distribute unto the poor, and thou shalt have treasure in heaven: and come, follow me. And when he heard this, he was very sorrowful: for he was very rich. And when Jesus saw that he was very sorrowful, he said, How hardly shall they that have riches enter into the kingdom of God! For it is easier for a camel to go through a needle's eye, than for a rich man to enter into the kingdom of God.

Jesus was nearing the end of His ministry on earth with only a few weeks left before He was to fulfill His destiny by dying on the cross. A rich young leader asked Him what he should do to inherit eternal life. Jesus answered him with the steps he needed to take and then went on to tell him that he lacked one thing: he needed to give his money to the poor and follow Him. It is interesting that Jesus uses the same words, *"follow me,"* that He did when He called Peter, James, and John to be disciples.

Matthew 4:19 And he saith unto them, Follow me, and I will make you fishers of men.

The young man went away discouraged because it would have cost him all his wealth. Some people think that Jesus was telling us that we should not have wealth. I see it from a different angle. I think that this rich young man would most likely have been the replacement for Judas, who handled the finances for Jesus' ministry.

Judas was the one who betrayed Jesus and later hung himself. This would have required the man to get through the things that had held him back. In his case, it was the love of money. The rich young man missed his destiny in God. He was afraid of losing his earthly possessions.

Luke 18:29, 30 And he said unto them, Verily I say unto you, There is no man that hath left house, or parents, or brethren, or wife, or children, for the kingdom of God's sake, Who shall not receive manifold more in this present time, and in the world to come life everlasting.

This young man may have suffered from Spiritual Identity Theft. He told Jesus that he had obeyed all the laws and felt that he was doing what was right. He knew there was a higher purpose in his life. Satan used a strategy of greed to hold him back from a greater destiny. With God there is always another chance! Many people never reach true fulfillment in life because they fall into some of the strategies I am going to reveal.

Again, as I begin to reveal the plans that Satan has against us, it is not meant to instill fear or to cause you to focus on negative things in your life. I will talk a lot about the ability to turn our focus away from negative things and toward God and his positive love and power to change our lives. I will also reveal some remedies that will help you to overcome the plans of the enemy and get you into a bright new future.

Chapter Fourteen
Identity Remedies

We need to develop a positive Kingdom perspective. God will reveal strategies to Breakthrough Spiritual Strongholds.

If you recognize any of these in your life simply pray and ask God to give you the strength and a remedy to overcome it. I have already given you some steps you can take, but now I want to give you strategies from God that you can implement into your life that will help build a solid spiritual foundation. When we continually focus our attention on things that are wrong, negative, or that don't work, then we can start to see the world through a negative viewpoint and start believing this is the reality everywhere.

Just watch the news on television and you can start thinking that things are very bad everywhere. Fear and hopelessness can set in, and we start thinking that the world is going down—so what is the use anyway? Well, the true reality is that God is still in charge and last I checked He is still in a good mood. His love and changing power are still available to us all.

We must develop what Jesus referred to as "eyes that see." We must have the belief that nothing is too difficult for God. God's love and power are much stronger than any demonic power. We have nothing to fear. It helps to get the perspective that powers of darkness in this world are trying to destroy God's creation. We must be careful not to buy into the lie that we are all doomed. So when we see someone suffering from things like depression, suicidal thoughts, or sickness, we must realize that this is not the will of God for this person or even ourselves.

It is the plan of the enemy to steal their life and destiny. Because God's love and will for us are the only true reality, we must recognize the works of darkness as a counterfeit and deterrent to God's intentions for us. We can learn a very powerful strategy in the encounters I just mentioned where Jesus encourages people to change their lives.

The example of Mary peering into the tomb of Jesus, crying while Jesus was behind her calling her to turn away from her pain. Satan wanted Mary to focus on her pain and loss but Jesus was calling her to focus on the new life that He brings. When you see the works of darkness in a person's life, or your own for that matter, you have the opportunity to positively turn it around and bring God's love and encouragement which will lead to a new life.

1John 3:8 He that committeth sin is of the devil; for the devil sinneth from the beginning. For this purpose the Son of God was manifested, that he might destroy the works of the devil.

I am always looking to encourage people who are suffering from negative influences.

Living our lives with a greater measure of God's love and light is extremely powerful. We dispel darkness, sometimes without having to say a word, because the Spirit within us is powerful and healing.

Ephesians 5:8 For ye were sometimes darkness, but now *are ye* light in the Lord: walk as children of light:

We all need to understand and regularly practice the positive spiritual principles of praying for those who curse us, loving those who hate us, giving to those in need, helping the oppressed, being humble as opposed to proud and arrogant, forgiving those who offend us the list is actually too long to fully mention here, but you get the picture.

Notice that most of these principles are relationally oriented. They teach us how to relate with others and with God. We can change the spiritual atmosphere around us by loving, blessing, and being an encouragement everywhere we go.

Many people love God, but when no one is looking, they can be guilty of mistreating or being mean to people.

Your life will be overflowing with good things that you gave out to others, to the point that you cannot help but change the world around you. What you sow is what you will reap. If you sow grumbling, doubt, fear, depression, anxiety, and complaining, then that is what you will get in return. Developing a positive Kingdom perspective and lifestyle is what will truly change our lives and the lives of many around us.

Seeing Ourselves as God Sees Us

The amazing thing about God is that when He sees your life He has a perspective that is way beyond ours. He somehow simultaneously looks at our past, sees our present struggles and knows our full potential in the future and He loves us right where we are today. He deals with us according to the level of maturity that we are at right now and He does not require more than we can handle.

Most of the strategies of Satan deal with the fact that we all sometimes let the past hold us back from the future. This is because we have not learned to develop the ability of seeing ourselves as God sees us. If you want to stop allowing negative things from your past to control your present and future, it will involve changing old thought patterns.

Romans 12:2 And be not conformed to this world: but be ye transformed by the renewing of your mind, that ye may prove what *is* that good, and acceptable, and perfect, will of God.

Renewing your mind involves replacing the old mindset with a new one. Your new mindset is who you are becoming, not who you have been. The good news is that this is the way that God sees you. When you come into line with God's intentions, you actually tap into His unlimited power to transform your life.

Here's how it works. God's purpose for you is to prosper you, give you hope and a future, and not harm you.

Jeremiah 29:11 For I know the thoughts that I think toward you, saith the LORD, thoughts of peace, and not of evil, to give you an expected end.

If you try to make changes in your life by focusing on what you should not do, then you are trying to live by rules and not by a relationship with God. God is relationship--oriented—that is why He refers to Himself as Father and to Jesus as His Son; this indicates that He wants to relate to us as family.

The Bible compares this transformation to stepping away from the picture of your old self and putting on a picture of your new self. God's focus is on you becoming who you were created to be. He relates to you according to this image. It is very important that you see yourself in this way as well.

Ephesians 1:18 The eyes of your understanding being enlightened; that ye may know what is the hope of his calling, and what the riches of the glory of his inheritance in the saints,

The Greek word used for "know" is to "see or perceive." This goes deeper than just head--knowledge. When you see and perceive the hope of your calling, it causes you to take action because it is much more tangible and real. God sees us as we are becoming or in other words, in our full potential. Here are some biblical examples illustrating this concept.

Judges 6: Gideon is hiding in fear, and an angel comes and calls him a mighty man of valor—God treated him according to the way He saw him in the future.

John 1:40-42 One of the two which heard John *speak,* and followed him, was Andrew, Simon Peter's brother. He first findeth his own brother Simon, and saith unto him, We have found the Messias, which is, being interpreted, the Christ. And he brought him to Jesus. And when Jesus beheld him, he said, Thou art Simon the son of Jona: thou shalt be called Cephas, which is by interpretation, A stone.

Saul was murdering Christians, and then God knocked him to the ground on the road to Damascus. Before Saul's life was changed, God told Ananias to tell Saul that he is a chosen instrument and is a brother. The key is to begin to see yourself in your full potential in God. See yourself as God sees you, not as you once were, or even as you are now, but by faith getting a picture of who you are becoming in God.

You might not be there yet, but if you begin seeing yourself there, then you will start changing your behavior to act differently. You will start coming into agreement with God for your life calling.

How to Change Instantly

You can change your behavior right now, instantly, when you understand that you can refocus your thoughts or emotional energy away from the negative. This is because whatever you focus on becomes your reality.

Proverbs 23:7 For as he thinketh in his heart, so *is* he: Eat and drink, saith he to thee; but his heart *is* not with thee.

Let's say you are focusing on feeling bad about being in debt—most likely you will carry this negative baggage with you throughout your entire life. It is like a weight tied around your neck and shoulders. Instead, decide right now that you will put a debt reduction plan in place and get on with life. Begin to refocus on finding creative ways to earn additional money and have fun in the process.

Galatians 6:7 Be not deceived; God is not mocked: for whatsoever a man soweth, that shall he also reap.

Matthew 21:22 And all things, whatsoever ye shall ask in prayer, believing, ye shall receive.

In other words, where you focus your energy, you are making this principle a reality in your life.

You can learn to make the most of every situation. Where your focus goes, your energy flows. It is not worth getting upset! As you learn to redirect your focus it will free you up to begin to plan how you want things to be instead. This is how your creative flow (connection to God) gets re-established and solutions to various issues in your life will come more easily to you.

Chapter Fifteen
Changing Your Current Situation

There are so many of us who have prophetic promises from God about operating at a higher level of ministry but are currently in a job or situation that we have little passion for.

Perhaps you need a financial breakthrough that will allow you to freely do all the things that God is calling you to. God spoke to me that a key for this breakthrough may lie in your current situation.

Change your situation

God wants to use your current situation to bless you and release finances and favor into your life. The key is learning to be content and working at whatever it is you are doing as if you are working for God Himself. This does not only pertain to jobs, but also to being in school, relationships or whatever situation you are in.

The Bible tells us that we can do incredible things through God's strength. Since God's love and power is limitless, what we can accomplish through His Holy Spirit has no limits as well. If we are unhappy and anxious about our situation, it can create limits to what we can do through God. Allowing God's love to flow through us, being content, and having gratitude can change the spiritual atmosphere around us and ultimately create an environment in which blessings are drawn to us.

Philippians 4:12, 13 I know both how to be abased, and I know how to abound: every where and in all things I am instructed both to be full and to be hungry, both to abound and to suffer need. I can do all things through Christ which strengtheneth me.

If you feel frustrated or stuck, begin to find good things in your life right now. Here are a few tips on how to change your current situation. Give thanks to God for all that He has done for you. Make a list of blessings and things you are grateful for. Learn to recognize and help draw attention to the good things in other people. Ask yourself, who can you encourage or help today? Who can you help practically?

Ephesians 3:20 Now unto him that is able to do exceeding abundantly above all that we ask or think, according to the power that worketh in us

We can begin experiencing a radical turn around in our spiritual lives and overcome Spiritual Identity theft when we simply go back to the basics of the things we believe, and find ways to make them a daily lifestyle. It is out of relationship and intimacy with God that everything will flow. Don't get me wrong, I still prayed and studied, but not at my fullest potential. It is amazing that you know this in your head, but getting yourself to do it makes all the difference. I began making Matthew 6:33 my guiding verse:

Matthew 6:33 But seek ye first the kingdom of God, and his righteousness; and all these things shall be added unto you.

The secret to spiritual growth

This is for every Christian to find the secret of growing spiritually. We can know the truth of the Bible, but if we are not actually doing it, then we are lacking a tangible revelation of the truth.

Once we get a revelation of any verse or principle, it becomes alive in us and gives us a spiritual push forward. If we take the revelation a step farther, and we do something to practically use it or apply it in our life, then we begin to advance. If we do it regularly and make a habit or lifestyle from it, then momentum kicks in and we go to an entirely new level that few people are aware exists. If you take it even further and show others how to do it, you move ahead even more in your maturity, and you gain more wisdom and anointing because the more you give, the more you will receive.

It really has been the secret to my success in my relationship with God and my ministry. Some people misunderstand these Kingdom principles and push forward, making them rules instead of relational opportunities to be a conduit for God. The difference between striving and actively pursuing is that those who strive do not have the revelation and are doing it out of motivations. When something becomes a rule, you lose intimacy with the giver of the gifts, and you begin to lack grace and love for yourself and others.

The principle of revelation is alive when God makes Himself real to us.

Revelations 19:10 And I fell at his feet to worship him. And he said unto me, See *thou do it* not: I am thy fellowservant, and of thy brethren that have the testimony of Jesus: worship God: for the testimony of Jesus is the spirit of prophecy.

Those who commit their lives to Christ through a revelation of God usually experience a much more fulfilling spiritual life from those who do it out of a decision based on guilt, logic, or rules.

Sometimes altar calls motivate people to come forward for the wrong reasons. When the Spirit draws us, as opposed to guilt or condemnation, then we connect with God at a much deeper level that is based on love, and we will see a greater level of change in our lives. I have had several very deep revelations of verses from the Bible that have changed my life and now the lives of many.

There are times for me when it is more and other times when it is less. The key is to grasp the revelation that things like reading the Bible, praying, worshipping, etc. help you connect with God because you are a temple of the Holy Spirit. When you connect with God through intimacy and relationship, then you will want to spend more time with Him instead of doing it because you have to.

Ephesians 1:17-19 That the God of our Lord Jesus Christ, the Father of glory, may give unto you the spirit of wisdom and revelation in the knowledge of him: The eyes of your understanding being enlightened; that ye may know what is the hope of his calling, and what the riches of the glory of his inheritance in the saints, And what *is* the exceeding greatness of his power to us-ward who believe, according to the working of his mighty power,

Ask God to give you eyes to see, ears that hear, and a spirit that perceives what it is He is calling you to right now!

Find Your Destiny

Destiny is what it is about. Many Christians fall short of fulfilling their destiny. I have been talking about destiny and life purpose and the fact that Satan wants to steal your spiritual identity to keep you from advancing and maturing. There are so many people today who are searching for the purpose for which they were created. A desire for purpose is rooted in our human nature. Too often, many of us try to fill this with things like careers, status, cars, or the perfect relationship or family. None of these are bad in and of themselves. However, they will not bring true fulfillment in life. Our purpose and destiny can ultimately only be filled through the good news of God's love.

Matthew 4:19 And he saith unto them, Follow me, and I will make you fishers of men.

Matthew 22:37-39 Jesus said unto him, Thou shalt love the Lord thy God with all thy heart, and with all thy soul, and with all thy mind. This is the first and great commandment. And the second *is* like unto it, Thou shalt love thy neighbour as thyself.

Matthew 28:19, 20 Go ye therefore, and teach all nations, baptizing them in the name of the Father, and of the Son, and of the Holy Ghost: Teaching them to observe all things whatsoever I have commanded you: and, lo, I am with you alway, *even* unto the end of the world. Amen.

Your destiny is a unique assignment from God that starts with learning to follow Jesus, loving God and others, and helping others to do the same. You cannot go wrong if you build your life on this foundation. I like to think of finding your life purpose or destiny as being similar to a "connect the dots" drawing.

At any given time your goal is to go to the next dot. Too often we want to rush ahead and we miss all the necessary growing opportunities that God has for us.

Destiny reveals itself over time and the more we pursue it, the clearer it becomes. In order to find your destiny it helps to understand that we all have been uniquely created by God and we all have a purpose.

1Corinthians 12:12, 13 For as the body is one, and hath many members, and all the members of that one body, being many, are one body: so also *is* Christ. For by one Spirit are we all baptized into one body, whether *we be* Jews or Gentiles, whether *we be* bond or free; and have been all made to drink into one Spirit.

We need to find our unique function and fit in life. Our purpose is intended to be fulfilled in who we are in God. We must allow God to renew our minds and our lives through His Spirit in order to fulfill our purpose among other Christians. Being in relationship and community with others is essential to our growth.

God has been leaving you clues about your destiny all your life.

Recognize and eliminate unhealthy habits. This may be a lifelong process but we all need to be motivated by God's Spirit and not our own desires. I had some bad habits of avoiding things I did not want to do. I also would do bad things when I got stressed out. I found ways to work through these patterns and now they no longer dominate my life.

Develop good new habits.

We can refocus our lives and renew ourselves by spending regular time reading the Bible and praying. We all know this but doing it takes effort.

Psalms 37:4 Delight thyself also in the LORD; and he shall give thee the desires of thine heart.

Matthew 6:33 But seek ye first the kingdom of God, and his righteousness; and all these things shall be added unto you.

Be generous. Be a giver. This is not just about money, although giving money shows where your heart is. Give your time, energy, affection, focus and attention to all that you do. If you need something in your life like wisdom, revelation, love, or money then you may want to try giving to others in the areas you need.

Whatever you sow you will reap. If we are not grateful then we will not recognize a blessing when it comes. Most people grumble and complain and they wonder why their life is full of negativity and bad circumstances. You can turn your life around today by dropping out of the grumblers club. Being grateful is a spiritual principle that allows good things to flow back to you.

I used to complain about the bad service I got on airlines, restaurants etc...

Learn to love. How we treat other people reflects our character. Godly character is required for all of us. How we love other people is most likely how we love God. Remember that love covers over a multitude of sins, love conquers all, and love never fails! You can check yourself on this and see if you are loving people. It starts with how you act behind the wheel of your car. For some reason we forget that the other car contains a real person. Don't let other people who are having a bad day drag you into their swirl.

Get to a place where you love others, pray for them and encourage them. You will have a lot more peace in your life. Develop a "breakthrough lifestyle." Most people live a lifestyle of avoidance. Instead, find things that you are putting off and do them. Even a small simple task, done daily or weekly towards what you feel called to do, may not look like much when we do them but they build over time.

Finding and fulfilling your destiny is not as hard as one might think. Build your life on a firm foundation that will allow you to accomplish all that God has in mind for you. Believe that you can do it! Look for things that ignite passion within you. Take small steps consistently.

Find someone who is doing what you want to do and study what they have learned. Do something today like read a book, do internet research, make a phone call, sign up for a class, or get some practical training. It is never too late.

Philippians 4:13 I can do all things through Christ which strengtheneth me.

We all need to make some types of changes in our lives. Positive change happens when you make a decision to do something and take steps to make it reality. Start small, stay consistent, and over time momentum will build. Transformation occurs when you go beyond your own strength of decision--making, tap into God's ultimate power and wisdom to renew your thinking and your behavior, and combine this with practicing the art of good choices. You can change your life, but transformation occurs when you practice things enough that they become automatic.

Transformation requires both God's power and your good choices. Most people either try to do it in their own strength and leave God out, or they focus entirely on being spiritual but fail to be proactive.

A really great thing about God is that He sees us as who we are becoming through His love and power. As He looks at your life, He knows your past, understands your present, and can see your future, all at the same time. His love, mercy, and grace are unfathomable. Imagine the possibilities if we could see ourselves the same way that God sees us. Much of the time we are not able to see our purpose and destiny with much clarity, so we are required to rely on faith.

The principle of faith allows us to trust that there is something special and unique for us, even if our experiences have been the opposite. Sometimes there is great resistance or even setbacks before we are able to get into the fullness of God's desires for us.

Hebrews 11:1 Now faith is the substance of things hoped for, the evidence of things not seen.

We need to be certain of the fact that God has nothing but good intentions for us, even though we may not see them yet. You'll see this in the powerful biblical principle:

Jeremiah 29:11 For I know the thoughts that I think toward you, saith the LORD, thoughts of peace, and not of evil, to give you an expected end.

These are God's intentions for us. His plans are to prosper us, to give us hope and a future. If you read on, you'll see the benefits of grasping this.

Jeremiah 29:12, 13 Then shall ye call upon me, and ye shall go and pray unto me, and I will hearken unto you. And ye shall seek me, and find *me,* when ye shall search for me with all your heart.

We must see what God is doing in our lives and work with Him to bring it about. It's time to take a stand against what Satan has in mind for us and come into line with God's wonderful intentions for us.

I have found that many people have the opposite in their lives. Instead of prosperity they have a poverty mindset and debt. Instead of living a life of confidence of no harm coming to them, they are living in fear. Instead of having hope they are hopeless, distressed, and even depressed. Instead of living a life with a clear vision, they have no clue about their destiny. And instead of seeing their prayers answered consistently, they often give up praying because they are discouraged.

These are all symptoms of Spiritual Identity Theft. If you have any of these negative things in your life you can turn them around today by asking God to remove the negative and bring His positive promises into your life.

Most of the time we forget to look back and see how far we have come. Or when God reveals a new strategy to you, be sure to write it down so you don't forget. It is good to make a habit of listing out things that God speaks to you. If He gives you a strategy then take some steps towards it. We don't know what to do next but there are other times when God is revealing it to us and we are not attentive to what He has said.

Proverbs 29:18 Where *there is* no vision, the people perish: but he that keepeth the law, happy *is* he.

Your Identity is in Christ

I want you to receive these next few Words for yourself. I am free from condemnation and have the strength to live my life free of despairing thoughts and the competing desires of my flesh. I am God's workmanship, created to do good works, which God has prepared ahead of time for me to accomplish. I am more than a conqueror through God who loves me. I have a clear mind and can make good decisions. I am increasing daily in faith, strength, wisdom, and love. I am able to love others because God has first loved me.

May God richly bless you on your journey and I want to encourage you to share what you have learned with someone else.

Chapter Sixteen
Satan's Open Door

Are you going through life and there always seems to be something you are dealing with. There is a door to our souls, a passage where our enemy can gain access. The presence of this portal goes undetected by many, but it is known widely in the realm of the spirit. This door stands partly open between light and darkness.

Under the divine law of God, our enemy is restricted to the realm of darkness. As believers, we are delivered from these powers of darkness. But if this door is opened, Satan and his cohorts are granted legal entrance. Their objective: to control areas of our lives. This Enemy Access always results in theft, destruction, and a loss of freedom. It can even mean our lives.

Matthew 16:18 And I say also unto thee, That thou art Peter, and upon this rock I will build my church; and the gates of hell shall not prevail against it.

Revelations 1:18 *I am* he that liveth, and was dead; and, behold, I am alive for evermore, Amen; and have the keys of hell and of death.

But how can we shut this gate to our lives, let alone lock it—especially if we are unaware of its existence? As a wise soldier, consider for a moment how your adversary thinks. Suppose you were an evil adversary with unrestricted and undetected access to a building. You come and go at will, slipping in to steal at whim. You enjoy your arrangement, so what do you do to insure your position and access to this building? How do you maintain your advantage? You go to great lengths to make certain the owner never detects your activity, for once your presence is discovered you are locked out.

This is exactly Satan's plan! If he can keep you ignorant, he retains his access.

Isaiah 5:13 Therefore my people are gone into captivity, because *they have* no knowledge: and their honourable men *are* famished, and their multitude dried up with thirst.

Ignorance comes with a high price. But we don't have to remain ignorant. If you live in a neighborhood where there are shootings every day would you forget to lock your front door? Of course not! Let's take it further. Would you dream of retiring at night with your front door not only unlocked but also left wide open? Absolutely not! The ludicrousness of it is almost offensive, yet countless people do this very thing. But it is not the door to a home that is left open—it is the door to their souls.

I've seen these unaware and unprepared believers from all walks of life, income, and culture. They are the educated and the ignorant. But they all have one thing in common: They are victims of a wise and cunning adversary who has placed them under his controlling curse. How? They left open the devil's door! This is not about witches and spells. Nor is it about the occult practices of astrology, palm reading, or Ouija boards. All these are blatant, evident invitations to the demonic realm. Most believers would never openly dabble in these. No, I speak of something much more subtle. It operates in the realm of oversight and ignorance. In this foggy arena, even believers fall prey.

This is not a new phenomenon or unique to our generation. It is as ancient as the devil himself. It is the iniquity that caused the fall of Lucifer, and displaced a third of the angels from heaven. It is rebellion, which is disobedience to God's authority.

You'd be surprised. Satan is not a fool. He and his cohorts are very cunning and crafty. Most believers do not dive willfully into disobedience; rather, they fall into it by way of deception.

Do you desire to protect and safeguard your home, life, and family? This is released as a warning to protect. It contains truths that expose deception and could save your life.

Days of Deception
We are in the days of deception where the enemy is looking to deceive us to leave the enemy full access to our lives. Satan is the master of deception. Jesus said he was not only a deceiver but also the very father of it.

John 8:44 Ye are of *your* father the devil, and the lusts of your father ye will do. He was a murderer from the beginning, and abode not in the truth, because there is no truth in him. When he speaketh a lie, he speaketh of his own: for he is a liar, and the father of it.

Jesus also warned us that his delusions and deceptions would become so strong in the latter days that if it were possible even the elect would fall prey to them.

Matthew 24:24 For there shall arise false Christs, and false prophets, and shall shew great signs and wonders; insomuch that, if *it were* possible, they shall deceive the very elect.

2Corinthians 11:2, 3 For I am jealous over you with godly jealousy: for I have espoused you to one husband, that I may present *you as* a chaste virgin to Christ. But I fear, lest by any means, as the serpent beguiled Eve through his subtilty, so your minds should be corrupted from the simplicity that is in Christ.

Paul compared a believer's vulnerability to deception with the deception of Eve. Eve was beguiled into disobedience.

Genesis 3:13 And the LORD God said unto the woman, What *is* this *that* thou hast done? And the woman said, The serpent beguiled me, and I did eat.

But it was a different story with Adam. "Adam was not deceived"

1Timothy 2:14 And Adam was not deceived, but the woman being deceived was in the transgression.

Romans 5:19 For as by one man's disobedience many were made sinners, so by the obedience of one shall many be made righteous.

Eve was beguiled into disobedience, but Adam knew exactly what he was doing.

I have watched some people in the church transgress God's commands with their eyes wide open, fully aware of what they are doing. They are not deceived—they are committing spiritual suicide. These people are difficult to reach. But the majority of the disobedient, like Eve, are deceived through ignorance. My cry is for these oppressed ones. Through knowledge of the truth, the enemy can be shut off.

Distorting God's Word

So let's look at how Satan could deceive Eve. Eve did not seem like a person who should have been susceptible to deceit. She lived in an entirely perfect environment. She had never been abused by an authority. There was no bad experience with a father, boss, or minister. She lived in a flourishing garden free of demonic influence or oppression. She'd known only God's goodness and provision as she walked and talked in His presence. So how was the serpent able to deceive her?

Genesis 2:16, 17 And the LORD God commanded the man, saying, Of every tree of the garden thou mayest freely eat: But of the tree of the knowledge of good and evil, thou shalt not eat of it: for in the day that thou eatest thereof thou shalt surely die.

It is God's very essence to love and give. He desired companions in His garden that would love and obey Him. He did not want a people without the freedom of choice. He longed for children made in His image with a free will. When He restricted their access to the tree He provided a choice that protected them from death. It involved their will: Would they trust and obey? Without a command there is no choice.

Genesis 3:1 Now the serpent was more subtil than any beast of the field which the LORD God had made. And he said unto the woman, Yea, hath God said, Ye shall not eat of every tree of the garden?

The serpent ignored God's generosity and emphasized the exception, thus implying that something was being withheld from Eve. With a single question he distorted God's protective command into an unjust denial of good. Can you hear the sneer in his voice as he questioned, "So, God said you can't eat from every tree?" He made God out to be a taker, not the giver He is. Satan led Eve down a path of reasoning where she would eventually question God's goodness and integrity.

Once he accomplished this, it was a small step to turn her against God's authority.

Attacking God's Authority

Most of us would never intentionally go against the authority of God but satan has a way of getting us too. Satan is sly; he was after the very foundation of God's authority. By causing the Lord to appear unjust, the serpent could attack God's dominion in Eve's mind.

Psalms 97:2 Clouds and darkness *are* round about him: righteousness and judgment *are* the habitation of his throne.

Though the woman corrected the serpent, the seed of doubt in God's goodness had been sown in her. Even as she answered, it is quite possible that she wondered about the goodness of God. I'm not sure why we can't eat from that tree. How could it harm us? What's in it that is so bad for us? With these newly raised doubts, she was open to questioning God's authority.

The serpent seized this opportunity to attack God's authority, truthfulness, and integrity by boldly contradicting Him. "You will not surely die. For God knows that in the day you eat of it your eyes will be opened and you will be like God, knowing good and evil"

Genesis 3:4, 5 And the serpent said unto the woman, Ye shall not surely die: For God doth know that in the day ye eat thereof, then your eyes shall be opened, and ye shall be as gods, knowing good and evil.

The master of deception undermined the foundation of Eve's loyalty to God and assured her she would not die. Then he quickly followed his contradiction with this reasoning: "Instead of dying you'll become more like God. You'll be wise and able to choose for yourself between good and evil. Therefore you will no longer be subject to Him or His unfair commands."

Eve was shocked! She now wondered, is this why God kept this fruit from me? She looked at the tree again but this time in a different light. She gazed at what was withheld from her. She judged the fruit to be good and pleasant, not bad and injurious. She reasoned, surely it is desirable and will make us wise. Why should I deny myself fruit that is so good for us?

This reasoning blinded her to all else around her. She forgot the abundant goodness and focused on the lone tree. She thought, God has kept this from us. It could have been ours all along. Why has He done this? What else has He withheld from us?

With the foundation of God's character, integrity, and goodness in question, there remained no reason to submit to His authority. Self-will or rebellion was the next step. Eve plucked the fruit, ate it, and gave some to her husband.

Immediately their eyes were opened. They were naked. Their disobedience brought spiritual death. By going against God's word and submitting to Satan, they opened satan's door, and he became their new master. They granted him not only access to their lives but also entrance into the world. Paul explained it this way:

Romans 5:12 Wherefore, as by one man sin entered into the world, and death by sin; and so death passed upon all men, for that all have sinned:

This act of disobedience conceived destruction, sin, and sickness—a list that has multiplied and grown more foul with each passing generation. Their rebellion opened wide the door to Satan's dominion and destruction. He took full advantage of his opportunity to be like God but not subject to Him. By enslaving God's creation, he enthroned himself.

Satan's mode of operation differs little today.

He still desires to pervert God's character in order to turn us against His authority.

James 1:16, 17 Do not err, my beloved brethren. Every good gift and every perfect gift is from above, and cometh down from the Father of lights, with whom is no variableness, neither shadow of turning.

It must be settled in your heart that there is nothing good outside the realm of God's will. James shows that you can be deceived if you believe there is good outside of God's provision. Consider carefully our discussion. No matter how good it looks, tastes, or feels no matter how rich, abundant, wise, or successful it will make you if it is not from God, it will eventually lead to intense sorrow and end in death. Each and every perfect and good gift is from God. There is no other source. Embrace this truth and settle it in your heart. Don't let looks deceive you! If Eve had followed this warning she never would have been swayed. But instead, she looked beyond the realm of God's provision to fulfill her desires.

How many people today marry the wrong person for the wrong reasons? God may have warned them through their parents or pastor, or showed them in their own hearts that they were making a wrong choice. But their own reasoning soon drowned out these other voices because the person they desired seemed good for companionship, pleasant to their eyes, and appeared to be wise in helping them make decisions. Ultimately they chose their will over God's. Later they suffer greatly for their misjudgment.

Many people disobey the will of God because they are enticed by the good and pleasant. Perhaps it is a means of prosperity or success outside the counsel of God's Word. They pursue their own desires and find fun, happiness, or excitement for a season. They find good in what God had said no to. They think God withholds all the attractive or fun stuff from them! They think He doesn't understand their needs and ignores the importance of their desires. They believe God is unfaithful because He doesn't answer their prayers when they expect Him to answer them. Reasoning questions, why wait for God's answer? Take the good and pleasant now! Two Situations, Two Different Responses Consider Jesus. He was in the desert for forty days and nights. He had gone without water, food, and comfort. Hunger returned because His body was close to starvation. If He didn't have food and water soon He'd die. But which came first—the provision or the temptation?

At this point Satan came to tempt Him,

Matthew 4:3 And when the tempter came to him, he said, If thou be the Son of God, command that these stones be made bread.

Just as with Eve, Satan questioned what God had said forty days earlier when He openly declared Jesus to be His Son at the banks of the Jordan.

Satan attempted to distort God's character. "Why has He led You out here to starve? Why doesn't He provide for You? Perhaps it is time You begin to provide for Yourself. If You don't get nutrition soon You'll die or end up with severe permanent physical problems. Use Your authority to serve Yourself. Turn this stone to bread."

The children of Israel faced this same dilemma after they left Egypt and followed God into the wilderness: they ran out of food. After a mere three days, they thought God had abandoned them to die. So they began to complain. They reasoned it was better for them to have died as slaves under the oppression of the Egyptians. At least they had food there. They thought God had tricked them by leading them out into the wilderness to starve. In their eyes, God was holding out on them. How deceived they were!

The attitude in the dessert was easily deceived into not submitting to His authority. This attitude would later cost them the Promised Land. It led them into rebellion.

Unlike the Israelites, Jesus denied Himself and waited for God's provision. He would not allow the enemy to pervert the character of God in His mind. He knew His Father would provide for His needs. He would stay submitted to God's authority no matter how unpleasant it was for the moment. He resisted Satan's temptation to take matters into His own hands; then

Matthew 4:11 Then the devil leaveth him, and, behold, angels came and ministered unto him.

Who, in the days of His flesh, when He had offered up prayers and supplications, with fervent cries and tears to Him who was able to save Him from death, and was heard because of His godly fear, though He was a Son, yet He learned obedience by the things which He suffered.

Hebrews 5:7, 8 Who in the days of his flesh, when he had offered up prayers and supplications with strong crying and tears unto him that was able to save him from death, and was heard in that he feared; Though he were a Son, yet learned he obedience by the things which he suffered;

God heard Him because of His godly fear. He did not doubt God's goodness. In the face of great temptation and intense suffering, more so than any other had undergone, He chose to obey even though it meant suffering.

This kind of obedience and submission blocked all inroads of the enemy to His life. Satan had no access or entrance. The devil's door remained shut. Jesus lived in perfect obedience to His Father; therefore, He could testify on the eve of His death:

John 14:30, 31 Hereafter I will not talk much with you: for the prince of this world cometh, and hath nothing in me. But that the world may know that I love the Father; and as the Father gave me commandment, even so I do. Arise, let us go hence.

Jesus spoke of obedience when He declared that the ruler of this world, Satan, had found nothing in Him. Through perfect obedience to His Father, the door was kept securely shut against Satan. Jesus was found blameless!

Important Principles

1. Obedience keeps the devil's door shut, denying him legal access.

2. Disobedience throws the door wide open, giving him legal access.

These principles are easy to agree with but quite difficult to live out, especially in today's culture where lawlessness abounds. The message is extremely important to every believer.

Chapter Seventeen
The Sea of Fear

Fear is a hidden stronghold for literally thousands and it's time to break free today. Knowing the Father in our crisis is the missing link for intimacy for many in all relationships. Now I know that I also have to make choices to live, not just physically, but in confronting my own personal fears that keep me on guard in all of my relationships. But how do we continue to get others to believe that if they choose to live, love will become their lifeline?

How do we show others the way to untangle their personal entanglements that prevent them from being a source of love, warmth, and safety to their families?

We first have to recognize that, for most of us, we live in that Sea of Fear.

- Fear of intimacy
- Fear of wounds
- Fear of "what ifs"
- Fear of man
- Fear of what man thinks
- Fear of judgments
- Fear of failures
- Fear of being loved
- Fear of giving love

Admitting that we have fear is the first step toward healing. Even though over the previous years I had an encounter that changed my image of how I viewed love, my God reminded me of a few more entanglements that helped me realize *that healing life's hurts is a process.* But the process has to have its beginnings. The list of fears is an endless list that, if we continue to allow, will drown us.

The effects of living in the Sea of Fear on our relationships keeps us from our purpose in life; our purpose in life to believe we are loved, so out of that belief, we are able to love others. The majesty of God is a breathtaking experience. As my human spirit delighted in the magnificent beauty, and the age and uniqueness of each individual iceberg, I realized just how insignificant I have viewed myself to be. Like those icebergs, I believe that in choosing life, my purpose in this world is so significant that others will feel my love and be motivated to live their dream and live out their destinies.

Taking a risk to allow myself to be loved so I may be able to love was the beginning of my healing process. This was not the end, but rather the beginning of a journey that would take me and our family into the greatest adventure life could offer.

Final Questions

1. What are some of the fears (entanglements) in your life that cause you to live hindered by life situations? (Name your Sea of Fear.)

2. If you fear intimacy in your life, can you remember a time or hurtful event that caused you to emotionally shut down?

3. What are some of the negative behaviors or fears that you might need to unsnap your lifeline from?

Chapter Eighteen
Take Off Offense

I have seen this one Spiritual Stronghold stop Christian's right in their tracks. Offense is one of the leading reasons why people leave churches and ministries. Not just those who come in the doors and sit down, but pastors, teachers, etc. People in ministry are leaving at an alarming rate! I can only imagine what the percentage is for regular churchgoers.

I am personally convinced that once someone seriously offends you, unless you really guard yourself, it is like anything that person says or does to you is wrong.

Once that offense has been taken on by the offended, no matter what happens that person will see it through that offense and judge what is going on. That person constantly questions others' motives and can't trust them. Offenses become like fences or walls that we keep hitting our heads against until we deal with the situation. It's like we have a rubber band attached to our waists, and every time we try to move forward from that event, somehow we find ourselves in tears and pulling back to the place of betrayal.

An offense can be defined as anger, resentment, or the cause of displeasure. When someone does something or says something that hurts us, it's OK that we have a moment. Let's face it—that kids' phrase "sticks and stones may break my bones, but names can never hurt me" is a lie. Those things hurt! It hurts when people are mean to us. I think inside all of us we want to be loved, accepted, and wanted, and when we go through hurtful situations, we can get offended.

Forgive and Forget? We can't completely deny our emotions. However, it becomes an issue when we can't get past it—when we're constantly remembering the event. I remember asking God about the concept of forgiving and forgetting.

Finally, after years of struggling with this, the Lord spoke to me and said, "You will forget the emotions that surrounded it." Truthfully, I can tell you stories of things that really hurt me at the time, but when I choose to move beyond it and allow Him to bring healing to me, the emotions aren't as fierce. Telling the story about how my friends were mean to me in school doesn't bother me anymore because I let go of the offense and I forgot the emotions around it. I chose to forgive. I can tell that story like a survivor because I am one.

Unforgiveness is the root of not being able to see past the offenses we've had in our lives. The Bible talks a lot about unforgiveness. Be merciful, just as your Father is merciful. Do not judge and you will not be judged? Do not condemn, and you will not be condemned. Forgive, and you will be forgiven. Give and it will be given to you. A good measure, pressed down, shaken together and running over, will be poured into your lap. For with the measure you use, it will be measured to you.

Luke 6:36-38 Be ye therefore merciful, as your Father also is merciful. Judge not, and ye shall not be judged: condemn not, and ye shall not be condemned: forgive, and ye shall be forgiven: Give, and it shall be given unto you; good measure, pressed down, and shaken together, and running over, shall men give into your bosom. For with the same measure that ye mete withal it shall be measured to you again.

Colossians 3:13 Forbearing one another, and forgiving one another, if any man have a quarrel against any: even as Christ forgave you, so also *do* ye.

Hebrews 8:12 For I will be merciful to their unrighteousness, and their sins and their iniquities will I remember no more.

If God won't even remember their sins, why should you? God is very clear in His Word that if you don't forgive others, then He doesn't forgive you of your sins. If you want to be ready for Heaven, you have to let these things go.

The acts of the sinful nature are obvious: sexual immorality, impurity and debauchery; idolatry and witchcraft; hatred, discord, jealousy, fits of rage, selfish ambition, dissensions, factions and envy; drunkenness, orgies, and the like. I warn you, as I did before, that those who live like this will not inherit the kingdom of God.

While Jesus hung on the Cross, bitterly tortured, He chose to forgive those who murdered Him.

Luke 23:34 Then said Jesus, Father, forgive them; for they know not what they do. And they parted his raiment, and cast lots.

If Jesus could forgive all the carnage that He suffered on the Cross, then what right do we think we have to hold onto whatever hurt us? We don't have a right; we must let it go. No matter what we've gone through in our lives, we must choose to forgive, even if we don't want to. Our flesh wants to hold grudges. Our flesh wants to get even. But we must choose to let go of the offenses.

Beware of Bitterness

Often we think if we hold onto a grudge then we're really hurting the people who hurt us. But in fact, holding onto a grudge just keeps us back and hurts us. We must forgive because that's what God wants us to do. We must forgive because we need to. If we're not careful, unchecked unforgiveness can turn into bitterness and cause us to be critical of every little thing.

All too often, people sit around in their homes after church and begin to verbally criticize and attack the pastor about the service, the sermon, the way he did or didn't look at them, or the way Sister So-and-So ignored them, and it becomes a downward spiral. This is not uplifting to your pastor or church, it's cursing it! If left unchecked, these people can become like a cancer to the church they are in. Whether they are aware of it or not, they are destroying the work of God from the inside out.

The Bible warns us all of guarding ourselves against bitterness. Don't pick on people, jump on their failures, criticize their faults—unless, of course, you want the same treatment. That critical spirit has a way of boomeranging. It's easy to see a smudge on your neighbor's face and be oblivious to the ugly sneer on your own. Do you have the nerve to say, "Let me wash your face for you," when your own face is distorted by contempt? It's this whole traveling road-show mentality all over again, playing a holier-than-thou part instead of just living your part. Wipe that ugly sneer off your own face, and you might be fit to offer a washcloth to your neighbor.

Matthew 7:1-5 Judge not, that ye be not judged. For with what judgment ye judge, ye shall be judged: and with what measure ye mete, it shall be measured to you again. And why beholdest thou the mote that is in thy brother's eye, but considerest not the beam that is in thine own eye? Or how wilt thou say to thy brother, Let me pull out the mote out of thine eye; and, behold, a beam *is* in thine own eye? Thou hypocrite, first cast out the beam out of thine own eye; and then shalt thou see clearly to cast out the mote out of thy brother's eye.

So where does that leave you when you criticize a brother? And where does that leave you when you condescend to a sister? I'd say it leaves you looking pretty silly—or worse. Eventually, we're all going to end up kneeling side by side in the place of judgment, facing God. Your critical and condescending ways aren't going to improve your position there one bit.

Romans 14:10-12 But why dost thou judge thy brother? or why dost thou set at nought thy brother? for we shall all stand before the judgment seat of Christ. For it is written, *As* I live, saith the Lord, every knee shall bow to me, and every tongue shall confess to God. So then every one of us shall give account of himself to God.

We're not in charge of how you live out the faith, looking over your shoulders, suspiciously critical.

2Corinthians 1:24 Not for that we have dominion over your faith, but are helpers of your joy: for by faith ye stand.

Live creatively, friends. If someone falls into sin, forgivingly restore him, saving your critical comments for yourself. You might be needing forgiveness before the days out. God said warn them against religious nitpicking, which chips away at the faith. It just wears everyone out.

Concentrate on doing your best for God, work you won't be ashamed of, laying out the truth plain and simple. Stay clear of religious talk that is only talk. Words are not mere words, you know. If they're not backed by a godly life, they accumulate as poison in the soul.

Religious, critical nitpicking just chips away at your faith and the faith of those around you. You have to be careful of the company you keep. While you might be at peace with a situation, if you continue to spend time with people who are still trying to get over something and you are constantly listening to them struggling with it, it can continue to conjure the emotions that you are trying to get past. It's harder for you to move forward if you are constantly being reminded of the issue. It's like running with ankle weights on. You'll grow tired and eventually it will drag you down.

I learned a long time ago to try to separate what people do from their motives. If God gives such attention to the appearance of wildflowers—most of which are never even seen—don't you think He'll attend to you, take pride in you, do His best for you? What I'm trying to do here is to get you to relax, to not be so preoccupied with getting set free, so you can respond to God's giving. People who don't know God and the way He works fuss over these things.

It isn't worth it to get so bent out of shape over the small things in life. Take a deep breath. Sadly, little things like this can cause the worst strife and divisions amongst friends and family. In the end, does it really matter? It was an accident; move on. Don't sweat the small stuff!

Don't Get Even
It's an easy thing to the flesh to want to get even with someone. It's easy to take this approach in life. When someone is getting to you, it's a common thing to want to get them back. However, when you get into this cycle, which is going to draw the line? If each payback gets worse and worse, when will it end?

The Bible teaches us that vengeance is God's. God sees when you've been wronged. He's not turning the other way. He knows when things happen. While the sin is not His will, He's looking to see how you react. He's looking to see what you do with the situation.

Romans 8:28 And we know that all things work together for good to them that love God, to them who are the called according to *his* purpose.

God has a way of bringing about all things for good. He has a way of making it OK even though the situation wasn't so good. You have to allow yourself to be free from the bondage of criticism. You must be free from bitterness. You must be free from unforgiveness. There have been many times I've cried out to God, saying, "But God, I just don't know how to forgive so and-so for what they did." Every time, He's shown me how to let it go. Ask Him for help to let go and forgive the person. His help is always the best!

Forgive

I believe that forgiveness is a process. You might be able to release some offenses right away, but some offenses hurt deeper. When the spasm of remembrance begins to hit you and your eyes start to water with tears, remember—ask the Lord to help you let it go.

In order for God to turn around what happened in your life, you have to let Him. You have to let go and let God take these situations. You aren't going to be able to do it on your own. You have to continually say, "I need Your help with this." I believe that you'll gradually see the pain and rejection won't be as bad. It'll lessen day by day. People who are survivors of horrific ordeals are usually able to tell their survival stories. They are no longer weighed down by bitter emotions. Because they've told their story so many times, they've healed in the process. You must choose to be a survivor. Choose to be the voice of the healed. Jesus came to set the captives free.

Isaiah 61:1-3 The Spirit of the Lord GOD *is* upon me; because the LORD hath anointed me to preach good tidings unto the meek; he hath sent me to bind up the brokenhearted, to proclaim liberty to the captives, and the opening of the prison to *them that are* bound; To proclaim the acceptable year of the LORD, and the day of vengeance of our God; to comfort all that mourn; To appoint unto them that mourn in Zion, to give unto them beauty for ashes, the oil of joy for mourning, the garment of praise for the spirit of heaviness; that they might be called trees of righteousness, the planting of the LORD, that he might be glorified.

If you want oil instead of ashes, if you want praise instead of mourning, if you want to be an oak of righteousness, then you have to allow God to take the pain and hurt of what happened and make something good out of it. You are not in control of your circumstances. Things happen in life, but you can surrender control to God. He always takes better care of the situations than you ever could.

If people are really mature in the Lord and you're friends, you should be able to go to them and discuss matters. While you may never agree on something or see eye-to-eye on it, talking about it can allow the communication to open up between you.

Oftentimes, our perceptions of what's going on aren't entirely accurate. By talking about it, we are able to figure out how much of the scenario is truth and how much of it is our perception.

We realize the conflict is there, but our perceptions of what others are thinking run wild, so instead of dealing with it, we avoid it. This is why many people just leave a church or end friendships—it's a result of what we think someone might think.

Repent for being bitter and critical in your church. Forgive people for whatever they've done to you. Choose to let it go. Stop running into the bathroom crying when things happen—you have to face it. Seriously, don't blame me for the issues you've gone through. Be aware that it's not my words that have hurt you, but it's the offense-colored glasses which you are wearing. Choose to take the glasses off and don't put them on again. Choose to stop looking at everyone and everything like they're getting ready to hurt you. Choose to move past your past and into your future. Aren't you tired of continuing to come back to that same hurt in your life? Aren't you tired of being bound by what happened to you? Cut the rubber band and get rid of the glasses. It's time you start being free from offense. Some of you are thinking, but you don't know what I've been through. You're right I don't, but God does. Give it to Him. It's time for you to stop being stuck on the things and move on.

I've learned in life that I can't affect everyone around me. I won't be able to change them; it's their choice. But I can affect me. I can change me. I can choose to stop getting offended. I can choose to be free from the bondage of offense. I can choose to pray for those around me. I have to choose to move forward even if those around me don't.

Chapter Nineteen
Rebellion is Witchcraft

If you think this Chapter has nothing for you don't skip through it. If you are reading this book you are in need of breakthrough and this Chapter addresses another stronghold you need to make sure you overcome.

The word WITCHCRAFT conjures up images of women in black, reciting incantations, traveling by broom, and scanning the future via a crystal ball while their cauldron simmers on the fire. Or perhaps the more modern view is one who casts spells and curses upon others for influence or gain. Let's leave behind both of these concepts and discover the heart of witchcraft, no matter what form it takes.

Samuel identified witchcraft in the life of Saul when he told Saul:

1Samuel 15:22, 23 And Samuel said, Hath the LORD *as great* delight in burnt offerings and sacrifices, as in obeying the voice of the LORD? Behold, to obey *is* better than sacrifice, *and* to hearken than the fat of rams. For rebellion *is as* the sin of witchcraft, and stubbornness *is as* iniquity and idolatry. Because thou hast rejected the word of the LORD, he hath also rejected thee from *being* king.

Notice Samuel directly linked rebellion with witchcraft, "For rebellion is as the sin of witchcraft."

The Hebrew word used here for witchcraft is qesem. Its English coun- terparts are divination, witchcraft, and sorcery. However, experts say the exact usage of these words in reference to occultism is unknown. This accounts for the various translations of the word witchcraft. The importance lies not in the label but in the result of witchcraft. This text should read, "For rebellion is witchcraft." This clarifies the context of this scripture. It is one thing to liken rebellion to witchcraft, but it is an entirely different issue to say it actually is witchcraft. Obviously a true Christian would never practice witch-craft knowingly. But how many today are under its influence because of the deception of rebellion?

Witchcraft in any form has the same result: it directly opens one up to the demonic realm. Its goal is to control circumstances, situations, or people. This is accomplished through various avenues often without the participant's understanding of what is happening in the spirit realm. Consciousness ranges from total ignorance of what one is doing to a complete understanding and awareness of the powers of darkness involved.

The goal of witchcraft is to control, but inevitably the controller becomes the controlled due to involvement with the demonic realm.

Rebellion Opens the Door

Many high school students dabble in the occult to various degrees. Youth group leaders regularly report encounters with classmates who were involved in witchcraft.

I learned that when an individual was initiated into a coven (a group practicing witchcraft), the leaders compelled him or her to take drugs, drink, engage in illicit sex, steal, and commit various other acts that defied the laws of God and our land. I was uncertain why this was encouraged until God opened the truth to me that "rebellion is witchcraft." By rebelling against the laws of God, their parents, and their society, the participants either knowingly or unknowingly grant legal access to the controlling demonic realm. Why? Rebellion is witch-craft. The more they rebel, the more they give legal right for demonic powers to influence and control them.

You may be wondering why I used the term legal right. That's because God has ordained laws of order in the spiritual realm. Under the divine law of God, the devil's authority has been restricted to the realm of darkness. Disobedience to God's authority, whether direct or delegated, moves a person out of spiritual light and into spiritual darkness where the enemy has legal access.

1Thessalonions 5:5 Ye are all the children of light, and the children of the day: we are not of the night, nor of darkness.

Matthew 6:24 No man can serve two masters: for either he will hate the one, and love the other; or else he will hold to the one, and despise the other. Ye cannot serve God and mammon.

Those who willfully commit themselves to the service of Satan understand this principle, yet others are deceived. These others are ignorant and mistake lawlessness for liberty, so they rebel claiming they are free. But there is no freedom in rebellion.

The New Testament reveals a clear picture of what actually takes place. The rebellious become slaves to depravity. Peter exposed their error this way:

2Peter 2:18, 19 For when they speak great swelling *words* of vanity, they allure through the lusts of the flesh, *through much wantonness*, those that were clean escaped from them who live in error. While they promise them liberty, they themselves are the servants of corruption: for of whom a man is overcome, of the same is he brought in bondage.

The truth is evident. There is no freedom but instead bondage and control in rebellion. It is the opening of the soul to demonic oppression and control. Paul re-emphasized this point:

Don't you realize that you can choose your own master? You can choose sin (with death) or else obedience (with freeing). The one to whom you offer yourself—he will take you and be your master and you will be his slave.

Romans 6:16 Know ye not, that to whom ye yield yourselves servants to obey, his servants ye are to whom ye obey; whether of sin unto death, or of obedience unto righteousness?

Resist Through Submission

Cain had the choice to honor God's will and close the door to sin's demonic control (witchcraft), or he could honor his own will in rebel-lion and welcome the crouching form of sin that sought to master (control) him

Genesis 4:7 If thou doest well, shalt thou not be accepted? and if thou doest not well, sin lieth at the door. And unto thee *shall be* his desire, and thou shalt rule over him.

How was Cain to close the door? The New Testament tells us:

James 4:6, 7 But he giveth more grace. Wherefore he saith, God resisteth the proud, but giveth grace unto the humble. Submit yourselves therefore to God. Resist the devil, and he will flee from you.

As we resist the devil by submitting to God, we close tight our door to the enemy. Submission is obedience. It is not limited to actions alone but also encompasses the realm of the heart.

Many try resisting the devil by quoting scriptures and praying fervently, and this is a legitimate form of spiritual warfare. However, some people do this yet remain disobedient to God's authority in other areas. When this is the case, the devil just laughs. Their disobedience has granted him legal access, and he is a legalist. They can bind and loose till they are blue in the face, but the sad fact remains that their lack of submission overrides the words they vainly speak.

Cain's downfall progressed this way: First, he harbored an offense against his brother. Hatred entered his heart, then deception, which paved the way for murder. When sin entered Cain's life, it caused him to do what he never could have imagined doing. If, as a young man, he had been told, "One day you will murder your brother," he probably would have responded, "You're crazy. I could never do such a thing." Yet he did. Why?

Disobedience had opened the door of his soul to sin, and it mastered him.

Rebellion also opened Saul's soul to the influence of a controlling spirit, which caused him to behave in a manner he never would have when he was in his right mind. The Bible indicates that it was not long after his rebellion that an evil tormenting spirit came upon his life and troubled him.

1Samuel 16:14 But the Spirit of the LORD departed from Saul, and an evil spirit from the LORD troubled him.

This evil spirit manipulated his life from that point on. There was no deliverance for Saul because there was no repentance from his sin. Saul became a very different man from the one we first met. He had been ordinary before he was king. He obeyed his father and respected the things of God. If you had approached him then and fore-told, "Saul, the day will come when you will kill eighty-five innocent priests, their wives, and their children in a fit of rage," he would have dismissed you as crazy and countered with, "I could never do that!"

The sad truth is he did,

1Samuel 22:17, 18 And the king said unto the footmen that stood about him, Turn, and slay the priests of the LORD; because their hand also *is* with David, and because they knew when he fled, and did not shew it to me. But the servants of the king would not put forth their hand to fall upon the priests of the LORD. And the king said to Doeg, Turn thou, and fall upon the priests. And Doeg the Edomite turned, and he fell upon the priests, and slew on that day fourscore and five persons that did wear a linen ephod.

That evil spirit caused him to live a life of jealousy, anger, hatred, strife, murder, and deception. It legally controlled him by way of his unrepentant rebellion.

Keep the Right Focus

Because we're discussing witchcraft, I want to warn you about a deception that happens to believers who are often trying their hardest to frustrate Satan.

The Bible says we are to keep our eyes on Jesus, the author and finisher of our faith.

Hebrews 12:2 Looking unto Jesus the author and finisher of *our* faith; who for the joy that was set before him endured the cross, despising the shame, and is set down at the right hand of the throne of God.

Focus on Jesus! If the devil gets in the way, resist him fervently and continue your pursuit of Jesus.

If we focus on evil and the occult, we are eventually ensnared by its seduction. What you focus on becomes your source of direction, and if your focus is steered off course long enough, it becomes your destination.

Lawlessness

John 5:30 I can of mine own self do nothing: as I hear, I judge: and my judgment is just; because I seek not mine own will, but the will of the Father which hath sent me.

Jesus had the Spirit of God without measure.

John 3:34 For he whom God hath sent speaketh the words of God: for God giveth not the Spirit by measure *unto him*.

From the testimony of John we discover the reason Jesus was filled with the Spirit of God without measure. He only did and only spoke the will and words of His Father. His perfected obedience gave Him complete fullness of the Spirit, for our God gives His Holy Spirit to those who obey Him!

Acts 5:32 And we are his witnesses of these things; and *so is* also the Holy Ghost, whom God hath given to them that obey him.

To be self-willed, doing and saying whatever you will, is rebellion, and rebellion is witchcraft. Just as Jesus was filled with the Spirit of God without measure due to His perfect obedience, perfect disobedience brings demonic influence without measure. This is seen in the life of the Antichrist. Scriptures refer to him as the lawless one.

2Thessalonions 2:8 And then shall that Wicked be revealed, whom the Lord shall consume with the spirit of his mouth, and shall destroy with the brightness of his coming:

He is described as the one,

2Thessalonions 2:4 Who opposeth and exalteth himself above all that is called God, or that is worshipped; so that he as God sitteth in the temple of God, shewing himself that he is God.

This verse has two levels of meaning. Yes, he will probably sit down in the physical temple of God. But he is also practicing perfect rebellion in his own body. Scriptures call our bodies the temple of the Holy Spirit. Why will the Antichrist have the power of Satan without measure? Because his rebellion is perfect and complete. Rebellion, remember, is witchcraft. It grants Satan legal entrance into a life. In perfect disobedience this man will carry the unchecked spirit of Satan.

2Thessalonions 2:9 *Even him,* whose coming is after the working of Satan with all power and signs and lying wonders,

This lawless one will be the very antithesis of our Lord and Christ. That is why he is called Antichrist.

1John 2:8 Again, a new commandment I write unto you, which thing is true in him and in you: because the darkness is past, and the true light now shineth.

Though this applies to every generation since John's day, it is a prophetic scripture that zeroes in to the final generation before the return of Christ. Peter, in writing about the last days, says,

2Peter 3:8 But, beloved, be not ignorant of this one thing, that one day *is* with the Lord as a thousand years, and a thousand years as one day.

One of God's days is equal to a thousand of our years. Divide one thousand years by twenty-four, and you have the amount of years for one of God's hours, approximately forty years. So when John says "last hour" he is referring to the final generation, which many believe is our own.

Notice the close of this scripture, "even now many antichrists have come, by which we know that it is the last hour." This man of lawlessness will not suddenly appear without warning or preparation. Before his appearance complete rebellion will seem common, since a large measure of lawlessness will already be at work in society.

The Mystery of Lawlessness at Work Today

In Paul's instructions to the Thessalonians, he talks again about the condition of lawlessness and rebellion prior to the revelation of the lawless one:

2Thessalonions 2:7 For the mystery of iniquity doth already work: only he who now letteth *will let,* until he be taken out of the way.

The mystery of lawlessness is the hidden principle that rebellion is witchcraft. This principle is already at work, and the lawlessness will progressively worsen until the man of lawlessness is revealed. This perfected rebellion will not come as a shock because the mystery of lawlessness has already been at work in our society and churches.

You may question, "Churches, too?" Yes, it is where the work of lawlessness is the most deceptive. In many ways the spirit of the world has crept into the church. Rebellion is increasingly becoming an acceptable way of life. There are many aspects of rebellion that is an indication of the coming end.

Matthew 24:12 And because iniquity shall abound, the love of many shall wax cold.

Most read this and think, "Sure, rebellion abounds in our society." Yet in this passage Jesus was speaking to Christians.

Matthew 24:10, 11 And then shall many be offended, and shall betray one another, and shall hate one another. And many false prophets shall rise, and shall deceive many.

The Greek word for love in this verse is agape. This Greek New Testament word is used to describe the love of God, which is found in believers of Jesus Christ. It is the love only He can give. The world does not possess this kind of love.

Jesus was saying, "Because disobedience will abound even among believers, the love of God in their hearts will grow cold!" The mystery of lawlessness (rebellion) seduces society and believers alike. It gives Satan and his cohorts legal access to our homes, churches, institutions and governments.

Many who are held captive will be set free as the oppression and deception of lawlessness are exposed. They will not remain captives of the devil to do his will. God will reveal the schemes of the enemy to those who truly love Jesus, and they will be delivered from his control.

2Thessalonions 2:10 And with all deceivableness of unrighteousness in them that perish; because they received not the love of the truth, that they might be saved.

Overcomers will embrace obedience and shun a self-serving life, for their delight is seeing God's will and purpose accomplished.

Chapter Twenty
The NEW Bride of Christ

Jesus paid the ultimate price for us all to become the NEW Bride of Christ. What love the Lord demonstrated by laying down His life for us, enduring the beatings and mocking of the people and bearing the wrath of God that we deserve. The Lord will receive His reward; He will be presented with a Bride that has been made ready for the marriage of the Lamb. The preparation of the Bride of Christ has been heavy on my heart lately.

What does she (the Bride) look like, what will it take for her to rise up and come into her fullness, to become the image of the Almighty?

Discovering our identity in Christ

Our identity is Christ. He is what we are called to be; His ways, thoughts, desires, and actions. We are to become like Him, He is our inheritance.

Galatians 2:20 I am crucified with Christ: nevertheless I live; yet not I, but Christ liveth in me: and the life which I now live in the flesh I live by the faith of the Son of God, who loved me, and gave himself for me.

We live so that the Lord can use us as living vessels that manifest His Kingdom on earth.

John 14:12 Verily, verily, I say unto you, He that believeth on me, the works that I do shall he do also; and greater *works* than these shall he do; because I go unto my Father.

If we could come to the realization of the power we have in Him, we would never fall into the lies of the enemy. The enemy sees what we will be when we step into the fullness of the Lord, and he will try and delay that as long as we allow him to. It is time for us to see as Jesus sees, and allow Him to step into us.

Allow the Lord to cleanse us

We are either going to allow the Lord to cleanse us or we will deceive our own selves. We can do that in part by fellowship with Him through extended times of communion. Sometimes sacrificing our time for Him is a big part. By limiting media an hour so we can spend that hour in His word and in prayer produces great dividends.

2Timothy 2:21 If a man therefore purge himself from these, he shall be a vessel unto honour, sanctified, and meet for the master's use, *and* prepared unto every good work.

How does a husband get to know his wife? By taking time away from the things around him and spending it with her to get to know her heart, her desires, and her passions. Our intimacy with the Lord must increase.

Isaiah 60:1, 2 Arise, shine; for thy light is come, and the glory of the LORD is risen upon thee. For, behold, the darkness shall cover the earth, and gross darkness the people: but the LORD shall arise upon thee, and his glory shall be seen upon thee.

The Lord needs a remnant of His people who will just be who we are in Him and allow Him to use us. It is time for us to step aside and let God step in.

Separate ourselves from the spirit of this world
The Bride of Christ will be set apart from this world and become the light of the world. It is not about what we say or preach, it is about how much of Christ is formed in us. When you carry a light into a dark room, that light overcomes the darkness and allows you to see. It is time for the church to overcome the darkness covering the world. The Lord is greater than all darkness put together, so imagine how bright things would be if we as the Body of Christ began to shine like Him. We must first seek the face of the Lord; to see him and become radiant.

Sensitive to God's voice
My sheep know my voice - We need to know when He speaks, to know His thoughts and desires. We must love the things He loves and hate the things He hates.

Proverbs 6:16-19 These six *things* doth the LORD hate: yea, seven *are* an abomination unto him: A proud look, a lying tongue, and hands that shed innocent blood, An heart that deviseth wicked imaginations, feet that be swift in running to mischief, A false witness *that* speaketh lies, and he that soweth discord among brethren.

What the Bride of Christ look likes
1. My perspective of the Bride is that we will provide the needs for those around us. Whether it is healing, deliverance, or discipleship; we are to provide for every need.

2. The body of Christ must be living testimonies of the spoken Word.

3. A remnant of people who are full of love, joy, peace, longsuffering, kindness, goodness, faithfulness.

4. We are to be overcomers. The bride will be victorious over the things of this world.

5. When I think of the Bride of Christ I think of a warrior who is covered in courage and boldness. Who trembles at nothing, who laughs at fear, a bride that is pure and spotless, and who walks in humility!

Attributes of Sons of the Kingdom

1. The Sons of God are to be anointed with the seven spirits of God.

Isaiah 11:2 And the spirit of the LORD shall rest upon him, the spirit of wisdom and understanding, the spirit of counsel and might, the spirit of knowledge and of the fear of the LORD;

2. Our inheritance is to become a Son of the Kingdom.

Romans 8:14, 15 For as many as are led by the Spirit of God, they are the sons of God. For ye have not received the spirit of bondage again to fear; but ye have received the Spirit of adoption, whereby we cry, Abba, Father.

It is time to cry out to our Abba, Father for Him to pour out His presence upon us. Oh what the day will look like when the body of Christ steps into the fullness of God; what light will begin to shine.

It is the heart of the Lord to see His Bride being a reflection of Him. He does not desire for us to live in fear, hopelessness, or sickness. He defeated those things when He overcame the grave. What is it going take for us to apprehend the victory that is ours? We are the victorious ones; we are to live with the Kingdom mindset here on earth as it is in Heaven.

The Lord wants us to have that now, not wait until we get to Heaven. Imagine the harvest we will bring in just by becoming the Bride of Christ.

Wedding

The beauty in a marriage is so powerful. The bride on her wedding day making herself ready for her beloved, dressed in pure white and jewels. She is ready to become one with her beloved. The joining together of a man and woman before God and all to see; making covenant with each other. Having one heart, one life; the power of two joining together in union as one; the wife receiving the name of her beloved. She will stand strong with Him, trusting in Him.

Ephesians 5:22-30 Wives, submit yourselves unto your own husbands, as unto the Lord. For the husband is the head of the wife, even as Christ is the head of the church: and he is the saviour of the body. Therefore as the church is subject unto Christ, so *let* the wives *be* to their own husbands in every thing. Husbands, love your wives, even as Christ also loved the church, and gave himself for it; That he might sanctify and cleanse it with the washing of water by the word, That he might present it to himself a glorious church, not having spot, or wrinkle, or any such thing; but that it should be holy and without blemish. So ought men to love their wives as their own bodies. He that loveth his wife loveth himself. For no man ever yet hated his own flesh; but nourisheth and cherisheth it, even as the Lord the church: For we are members of his body, of his flesh, and of his bones.

One Body and One Flesh

We are to be one body and one death. Just as the husband and wife are to be of one flesh, so is the Bride to be one flesh with Christ. The beauty of the lasting love between a husband and wife is such a reflection of the perfect love Christ has for His Bride.

There is no greater love than on the day Jesus died for us and rose again so that we could have a life free from sin, sickness, death, regret, shame, hopelessness, freedom from the lies of the enemy. He loves us so much that He took it all for us so that we could have a life of freedom. In Him we are free, no matter how hard things get or how dark the world may be, He is our safe haven. We are free in Him, and there is no darkness in all the earth that comes near to how great He is.

It is my prayer and hope that I will live a life that is pleasing to Him. That I am able to complete every purpose He has for me. To be made ready as His bride. To know who I am in Christ, to know my position and to stand strong in it. To walk in strength and courage; to laugh at fear; to be a reflection of His character, power, image, and His love. To just BE; to be a living vessel so that His kingdom can be manifested through me and to know Him through communion and intimacy with Him!

Revelations 19:7 Let us be glad and rejoice, and give honour to him: for the marriage of the Lamb is come, and his wife hath made herself ready.

But I know the Lord has a harvest to receive and a Bride to be made ready. It is our destiny to see that harvest brought in, so that Christ will receive the full reward for His sufferings.

He will have it; He will have His Bride that is pure and spotless.

Chapter Twenty One
The Valley of Brokenness

The most desperate message I've ever taught was on this powerful subject. The Lord is near to those who have a broken heart, and saves such as have a contrite spirit.

Psalms 34:18 The LORD *is* nigh unto them that are of a broken heart; and saveth such as be of a contrite spirit.

Multitudes of saints have fallen off the path of life. Their countenances fall of many Christians and they become fearful when I tell them that brokenness is necessary in the heart of *every* Christian. On numerous occasions, we have seen a change in their spirits that takes people to an unusual level of disappointment. God will be hindered if we do not embrace the Valley of Brokenness simply because He does not use prideful and arrogant people.

When we are walking in the cloud of pride, it will cause destruction to ourselves and others around us. If we were to put one individual who has pride, secret sin, or a spirit of lying in a large building, they eventually would find each other. These prideful, sinful, and lying spirits will come into contact and connect one to another some way or another. Pride goes before destruction.

Proverbs 16:18 Pride *goeth* before destruction, and an haughty spirit before a fall.

This is why we need the Holy Spirit to change us; when we need to cry out to God and plead the blood of Jesus in order to be better in our circumstances and lives, He will hear us, especially in our most hurtful and desperate times of trouble. When change begins with its cousin *Uncomfortable*, we start to rebuke and destroy the works of the enemy. Really God is doing it—honoring our prayers from the night before, asking Him to change us and our ways.

I have come to this conclusion; many of us really don't want to change for the better. Being comfortable is comfortable, and many of us do not want anything or anyone to remove us from our comfort zone. My inquiry is, how will God be able to do all these wonderful things for us and through us if we don't want to pay the price? Are we willing to pay the cost, or will we refuse to become broken?

One reason why many get fearful is because the process of becoming broken really hurts. It's better for us to humble ourselves than for God to do it.

James 4:10 Humble yourselves in the sight of the Lord, and he shall lift you up.

1Peter 5:6 Humble yourselves therefore under the mighty hand of God, that he may exalt you in due time:

When God does it, it results in suffering. Humiliation is part of humility. Love never fails, and it covers a multitude of sins. Prayer is very important in our lives. God loves us more than words can ever demonstrate. It will take eternity for God to show us how much He loves us, which is why we have to live in a body that never dies or gets old. Since God is eternal and His love is eternal, it's going to take eternity to show us His charity. His capacity to love is greater than ours, and His capacity to hurt is greater than ours. We have to submit and be humble in the sight of our God.

If we ask for brokenness in prayer, instead of allowing the Lord to do it, it will go well with us. Here are some passages that highlight the importance of humility:

1Peter 5:6 Humble yourselves therefore under the mighty hand of God, that he may exalt you in due time:

Psalms 34:15-19 The eyes of the LORD *are* upon the righteous, and his ears *are open* unto their cry. The face of the LORD *is* against them that do evil, to cut off the remembrance of them from the earth. *The righteous* cry, and the LORD heareth, and delivereth them out of all their troubles. The LORD *is* nigh unto them that are of a broken heart; and saveth such as be of a contrite spirit. Many *are* the afflictions of the righteous: but the LORD delivereth him out of them all.

Consecrate

Consecration isn't spoken about much from the pulpit these days. The word *consecrate* means, to make pure, holy, consecrate, set apart, devoting oneself to God, to regard as sanctification.

This is when we separate ourselves from the noise, devoting ourselves to God completely with our time, looking to see what God's will is for our lives. No whining and complaining about how lonely we are or how we need to be around people—this is between just us and the Spirit, walking in total subjection to His will and plan. We must come to God with humble hearts on a day-to- day basis. This is how we conquer the enemy. This is how we are able to meditate on His Word. This is how we become obedient and willing. If we do not humble ourselves and become broken, so He can pour out His anointing through us on an internal level, He will expose us and break us on an external level. That love process will be very painful and humiliating at times, but rewarding when it is over. Men and women who are specifically and specially commissioned will not have the luxury of fitting in with the world at great levels. There will be instances when people won't understand us if they do not have an equal relationship with the Father as we do. Others may misrepresent us. Some may oppose us, and we will find ourselves lonely many times. We will be the ones always looking for friends to hang out with, but they will not be looking for us.

God moves in stillness and in the quiet. Isaiah the prophet said that in quietness and in confidence will be our strength.

Isaiah 30:15 For thus saith the Lord GOD, the Holy One of Israel; In returning and rest shall ye be saved; in quietness and in confidence shall be your strength: and ye would not.

Learning to be still will help us know that He is God. When we are in spiritual training as ambassadors of Christ, we will need to have ears to hear what the Spirit is saying to *us*. There is no second-hand faith; we have to do this all alone, just us and the Holy Spirit. He will always point us to Jesus. As we remain in the quiet, we will start feeling a draw to spend more time with Him. In the wee hours of the morning, when He wakes us up to speak to Him and listen for His response, it will increase us in the Spirit.

I believe The Word of God is placed *on* our hearts, because after He begins to break us, His Word will fall right in without needing to force an entrance. The Holy Spirit is a gentleman. He does not force Himself on anyone. All we have to do is make sure we are right in the sight of the Lord by doing what He commands. We must love Him with everything we are, calling out His name in the good times and the bad times. Turmoil doesn't always have to be our last name. Jesus' name is above everything imaginable in all of creation.

We have music, lyrics, artistry, dance, and so much more that demonstrates our love to Him and for Him. When we get close to the Lord and we begin to have a deeper relationship with Him, we will learn when to speak and when not to speak. After we do all the worshiping and praising of the Lord, we need to set an environment to have quietness and stillness rule in our homes. Learning to wait on the Lord in the quiet helps us to endure through hardships and troubles.

Lamentations 3:26 *It is* good that *a man* should both hope and quietly wait for the salvation of the LORD.

Psalms 46:10 Be still, and know that I *am* God: I will be exalted among the heathen, I will be exalted in the earth.

Educating ourselves and building our character enables us to be able to listen, slow to speak, and slow to become angry when challenging issues arrive.

James 1:19 Wherefore, my beloved brethren, let every man be swift to hear, slow to speak, slow to wrath:

Broken, according to *Webster's Dictionary,* means, to be fractured, upheld, discontinuous, or interrupted. In a way this is true with God; when He decides to break us, we become fractured, broken, and interrupted in our everyday ways.

We will see situations—which we were looking forward to having fall into place—suddenly discontinued. Things will become dry, and people start falling away from us. Slowly, but surely, it *will* happen. Sometimes, it will not even come through us asking. When the Lord chooses to interrupt us, it will come to pass. However, this mainly happens when God is calling us or training us for ministry. We must always be in a place where we are able to listen to His voice while sensing His heart's desire for our lives. He is not a toy we play with any time we become bored and uninterested. Many unbelievers in the past have tested Him and have paid a high price. The owner of the Titanic stood on the bow, cursed God, and shook his fist to Heaven in doubt and anger, dictating to the Lord that He couldn't sink his ship.

For years, Christians have claimed they want to change their lifestyles, ways, or attitudes, but one thing they failed to realize is that if they haven't changed after all this time, as He has been pricking their hearts to change, it shows that they are not willing to go through the fire of brokenness.

We have to learn to trust God with all our hearts; He knows how to change us and mold us. Fear is not of God.

2Timothy 1:7 For God hath not given us the spirit of fear; but of power, and of love, and of a sound mind.

We must not let the devil stop us from becoming broken and poured out before God and other people. The Book of Psalms will help us to have a relationship with God by worshiping and praising Him correctly, and the Book of Proverbs will help us to have the wisdom to deal with other people.

We must guard our spirits or the enemy will have a field day with our minds and thoughts. Not every thought that comes into our mind is ours. The main ploy of the devil is to cast fiery darts (thoughts) into our minds in order to break down our faith. Fake Christians, who come to us in sheep's clothing, assuredly have polyester for wool, fangs for teeth, and paws for feet. In this age we are living in, we have to be aware and watchful of the counterfeits; sometimes they are not alone. They may even be among a leader in a church who is not well informed of their secret insolence, impudence, and trickery. We must be aware of these types of spirits in people while walking with discernment and a lowly attitude. We will always go further in the invisible when we do, manifesting into the natural for all to see Christ's Spirit radiating from us.

Chapter Twenty Two
When the Thief Steals

God loves to restore everything the enemy steals. Just begin to thank God now for His unending, immeasurable love for you and your loved ones.

We can nourish ourselves on the Word of God together, as we read a portion from the Apostle Paul's letter to the Ephesians church. Here we go.

Ephesians 3:14-21 For this cause I bow my knees unto the Father of our Lord Jesus Christ, Of whom the whole family in heaven and earth is named, That he would grant you, according to the riches of his glory, to be strengthened with might by his Spirit in the inner man; That Christ may dwell in your hearts by faith; that ye, being rooted and grounded in love, May be able to comprehend with all saints what *is* the breadth, and length, and depth, and height; And to know the love of Christ, which passeth knowledge, that ye might be filled with all the fulness of God. Now unto him that is able to do exceeding abundantly above all that we ask or think, according to the power that worketh in us, Unto him *be* glory in the church by Christ Jesus throughout all ages, world without end. Amen.

Oh yes! Oh, the love of God! The Lord is ultimately and intimately acquainted with you. He sees you, and He wants you to "know that you know" that He has not abandoned or forsaken you. He wants you to know at all times, especially in the dark hour of your soul, He is with you and He is the Great Restorer.

Joel 2:21-25 Fear not, O land; be glad and rejoice: for the LORD will do great things. Be not afraid, ye beasts of the field: for the pastures of the wilderness do spring, for the tree beareth her fruit, the fig tree and the vine do yield their strength. Be glad then, ye children of Zion, and rejoice in the LORD your God: for he hath given you the former rain moderately, and he will cause to come down for you the rain, the former rain, and the latter rain in the first *month*. And the floors shall be full of wheat, and the fats shall overflow with wine and oil. And I will restore to you the years that the locust hath eaten, the cankerworm, and the caterpiller, and the palmerworm, my great army which I sent among you.

Your barn walls are going to bust down! That's what God does. Biblically, that's what restoration looks like.

Increase and Multiplication
I've come to realize that when God restores, He brings an increase! When God restores, He multiplies! There is something about the "restoring nature" of God.

Job 42:10 And the LORD turned the captivity of Job, when he prayed for his friends: also the LORD gave Job twice as much as he had before.

In the Bible, we see that if harm came to someone or something was stolen, that God would command that the return be greater than what was plundered or robbed.

Exodus 22:1 If a man shall steal an ox, or a sheep, and kill it, or sell it; he shall restore five oxen for an ox, and four sheep for a sheep.

Exodus 22:4 If the theft be certainly found in his hand alive, whether it be ox, or ass, or sheep; he shall restore double.

Leviticus 6:5 Or all that about which he hath sworn falsely; he shall even restore it in the principal, and shall add the fifth part more thereto, *and* give it unto him to whom it appertaineth, in the day of his trespass offering.

Leviticus 22:14 And if a man eat *of* the holy thing unwittingly, then he shall put the fifth *part* thereof unto it, and shall give *it* unto the priest with the holy thing.

And it didn't stop at that point! There was a "seven fold" principle in connection with restoration (and vengeance) as well.

Proverbs 6:31 But *if* he be found, he shall restore sevenfold; he shall give all the substance of his house.

Today, I believe that God ordains it like this in the spirit. When the thief steals, he must give back sevenfold. When the devil comes to kill, steal, and destroy, God has set forever in eternity that you must get back sevenfold. And God will restore you in a better way than you were at first, and then He will increase and multiply what was stolen. That's our God because God is good. Listen. We need this revelation. For instance, when God wants to restore your anointing, it honors Him that you make a declaration like this: "He wants to give me a double portion of anointing!" When God restores, you are going to have double joy, everlasting joy, a double portion! He is going to bless you with an increase and command the thief to give back sevenfold.

If your marriage needs to be restored then stir up your faith and ask: "My God, please, I want You to restore my marriage, and I want it to be better than it was in the first place. I want there to be double the intimacy."

Get aggressive. Don't just settle for an "okay, restore my marriage" attitude. "Restore my marriage and give it to me double!" "Restore my finances and give it to me double!" "Restore my anointing and give it to me double!" We can ask God because of the nature of the restoration process of the Holy Ghost. He increases, and He multiplies.

For instance, when God heals my body, when God restores my body, I'm not just going to be healthy, I am going to have *divine health*. And then I'm going to minister healing to the sick because I am getting a healing anointing in the process. That's restoration! Listen to this: anyone that gives up houses, lands, brothers, sisters, possessions in this lifetime for the sake of the gospel, God will restore back one hundredfold now!

Mark 10:29, 30 And Jesus answered and said, Verily I say unto you, There is no man that hath left house, or brethren, or sisters, or father, or mother, or wife, or children, or lands, for my sake, and the gospel's, But he shall receive an hundredfold now in this time, houses, and brethren, and sisters, and mothers, and children, and lands, with persecutions; and in the world to come eternal life.

Ephesians 3:20 Now unto him that is able to do exceeding abundantly above all that we ask or think, according to the power that worketh in us,

We need to have a bigger vision! When we stand in faith and believe that God is hugely enthusiastic about wanting to bring restoration into our lives, we truly honor Him.

God's Purpose in Restoration

God wants to restore your life even more than you could ever want it. God wants you to know that He is extremely interested in accomplishing personal restoration in your life. His desire is that when you experience the blessing of personal restoration (and you will, so have faith), that yes, you will be blessed, but even more, that you will draw closer and closer into His heart. His biggest purpose for restoration is intimacy with you. Do you realize that without you, without your love and friendship, God is grieved? Think about that. You know, restoration is something supernatural.

After Jesus Christ died on the cross for you and me and we received Him as our Lord and Savior, He restored each one of us into personal relationship and fellowship with Him by taking our sins upon Himself and drawing us into His heart.

It's like we are restored in such a way that the experience that Adam and Eve had with God when He walked with them in the cool of the garden is also our experience to enjoy. His presence and His glory were there in the garden. The secret place of His presence is the "garden." Such restoration redeems, and it transcends time, space, and eternity. And this blessing is available for us today. What an important revelation to have. Yet, the choice is ours. We can actually choose to stand in faith, believing that God wants to restore to us the same kind of special intimacy that He enjoyed with Adam and Eve in the Garden of Eden. I don't believe that we have to wait for the day when we die and go to Heaven to enjoy these things.

Luke 17:21 Neither shall they say, Lo here! or, lo there! for, behold, the kingdom of God is within you.

From what I see in my Bible, Heaven for me began the day that I received eternal life. That is Heaven. We are the bride of Christ, whether we stand before God individually as His child, or collectively as the body of Christ. I want us to be an excited bride, anticipating the union, the oneness, and the intimacy that is reserved for us to take pleasure in, in Christ, with God. He desires to speak to us plainly as a friend speaks to a friend.

Exodus 33:11 And the LORD spake unto Moses face to face, as a man speaketh unto his friend. And he turned again into the camp: but his servant Joshua, the son of Nun, a young man, departed not out of the tabernacle.

John 15:12-15 This is my commandment, That ye love one another, as I have loved you. Greater love hath no man than this, that a man lay down his life for his friends. Ye are my friends, if ye do whatsoever I command you. Henceforth I call you not servants; for the servant knoweth not what his lord doeth: but I have called you friends; for all things that I have heard of my Father I have made known unto you.

To desire the presence of God above all else, and in a much greater way than our common thinking dictates--this brings God such great delight! Let's not let religiosity, man's tradition, or whatever denomination you were raised in, set limits for what you can or cannot receive from the hand of the Lord. There remains a rest in Him. Unbelief has kept us from walking in the full inheritance of everything that we can have in the spirit. I want you to get hungry for God; be more focused on being hungry for the manifestation of the glory of God, union, and intimacy. God opened the garden again!

Today, God is going to restore hope to you. So why not prepare your heart right now for what God wants to do in your life? We've just barely begun this New Year, the year of restoration, new beginnings, and intimacy with God. So, just as I opened this teaching about hope (from the Book of Joel), let's close it on the same note--HOPE. God is not going to disappoint you, and He wants your heart to embrace hope once again--the restoration of hope. Let such knowledge become a healing balm to your heart while you reflect on Paul's encouraging message to the Romans.

Romans 5:1-5 Therefore being justified by faith, we have peace with God through our Lord Jesus Christ: By whom also we have access by faith into this grace wherein we stand, and rejoice in hope of the glory of God. And not only *so,* but we glory in tribulations also: knowing that tribulation worketh patience; And patience, experience; and experience, hope: And hope maketh not ashamed; because the love of God is shed abroad in our hearts by the Holy Ghost which is given unto us.

It is time for you to allow the process of Breakthrough of Spiritual Strongholds. If you really want to be free God will finish the work He started in you.

About the Author

Bill Vincent was born 12/25/73 in Illinois. Bill had a lot of challenges as a child. Bill was the teenager parents didn't want their children to hang with. Bill was invited to a prophetic service about 1990 and after he went that was the service that changed his life. Bill was born again and ministered to for the first time. The man that prophesied to Bill that day was Dennis Goodell of International Miracle Ministries. Dennis Goodell has now gone on to be with the Lord.

Bill was a servant to Dennis Goodell for about ten years and had seen and experienced a great deal of miracles. This was the man Bill received an impartation of gifts of the Holy Spirit.

Bill was trained within the Church for many years. Bill's prophetic gift was matured and sharpened. Bill was ordained in 2001 while being a minister within the Church. Bill continued ministering in the Church and other places. In 2004 Bill established a Church in Litchfield, IL.

This ministry traveled as the Lord led. Bill operated in the prophetic with words of knowledge for healing spirit, soul and body. In 2008 Bill was frustrated and sought God for something fresh. After a couple of months God showed up with His mighty presence. August 2008 a Revival started. God's presence got stronger and stronger. After a few months God began to show up with mighty miracles, healing, signs and wonders. The revival continued for over two years. There were many miracles and signs every week. There were testimonies of Cancers healed, tumors removed, arthritis healed and many other creative miracles.

Bill has an accurate prophetic gift, a powerful revelatory preaching anointing with miracles signs and wonders following.

Bill started a ministry after many years of ministry by the name of Revival Waves of Glory Ministries in 2010. This ministry is a ministry with a fresh vision. God has brought Bill through much adversity. This ministry has had signs and wonders with deep prophetic ministry. Bill is a Prophet of God with a true Apostolic Anointing. Bill has authored many books, established a School of ministry called The School of the Supernatural and created a book publishing company called Revival Waves of Glory Books & Publishing.

Bill has found the glory of God in an awesome way. He has a special relationship with the father and powerful revelatory, healing and prophetic anointings.

Bill is married to his wife Tabitha who has two beautiful daughters. Bill and his family live in Litchfield, IL. Tabitha works closely with Bill in all the ministries day to day duties. I (Bill Vincent) am grateful every day to have these three amazing women in my life. Thank You Lord!

Recommended Books

By Bill Vincent

Overcoming Obstacles

Glory: Pursuing God's Presence

Defeating the Demonic Realm

Increasing Your Prophetic Gift

Increasing Your Anointing

Keys to Receiving Your Miracle

The Supernatural Realm

Waves of Revival

Increase of Revelation and Restoration

The Resurrection Power of God

Discerning Your Call of God

Apostolic Breakthrough

Glory: Increasing God's Presence

Love is Waiting – Don't Let Love Pass You By

The Healing Power of God

Glory: Expanding God's Presence

Receiving Personal Prophecy

Signs and Wonders

Ending Cycles of Pain

Signs and Wonders Revelations

Children Stories

Rapture Revelations

The Secret Place of God's Power

Building a Prototype Church

Breakthrough of Spiritual Strongholds

Glory: Revival Presence of God

The Watchman of the Lord

Overcoming the Power of Lust

Glory: Kingdom Presence of God

Children Stories 10 Book Series

Faith Bible Adventures

Transitioning Into a Prototype Church

The Stronghold of Jezebel

Healing After Divorce

A Closer Relationship With God

Cover Up and Save Yourself

The Watchman of the Lord 2

By Bill Vincent Spanish & French Translation

Love is Waiting – Don't Let Love Pass You By

Signs and Wonders Revelations

Breaking of Spiritual Strongholds

I Married Jezebel

Increasing Your Prophetic Gift

Receiving Personal Prophecy

By Bill Vincent, Paula Loveless, Joseph Basurto, Dawn Vitale and Jackie Money

Experience God's Love

By Bishop Gregory Leachman

God's Greatest Challenge:

Man & His Ungodly Ways

Conforming to the Mind of Christ

By Richard Money

My Life in a Salami Factory

Journey of Faith (EPOS Edition)

By Kevin Cann

Who Is Your Source

To Order:

Email:

billvincent@revivalwavesofglory.com

Web Site:

www.revivalwavesofglory.com

Mail Order:

Revival Waves of Glory

PO Box 596

Litchfield, IL 62056

Shipping $5.00

Prices do not include shipping and are subject to change. If you mail an order and pay by check, make check out to Revival Waves of Glory.

Most books are in multiple formats such as Hardcover, Soft-Cover, Ebook (such as Kindle & Nook), and Audio Books.

www.ingramcontent.com/pod-product-compliance
Lightning Source LLC
Chambersburg PA
CBHW030519080526
44586CB00011B/258